Reaching Beyond The Break

Reaching Beyond The Break

TRUSTING GOD WHEN THE ODDS OF
LIFE ARE STACKED AGAINST YOU!

Cornelius W. Dixon

Foreword By: Kawonnon Taylor
Author of "Treasured Gifts from Dark Moments"

Cornelius W. Dixon
2015

Reaching Beyond the Break
Printed in the United States of America
Copyright © 2015 by Cornelius W. Dixon

Scripture quotations are from the New King James Version *(unless otherwise indicated)*. Copyright ©1982, 1995. Used by Thomas Nelson, Inc. Used by permission. All rights Reserved. (www.cambridge.org).

Scripture quotations identified (KJV) are taken from the King James Version of the bible. Crown copyright in UK.

Scriptures taken from The Message (MSG). Copyright © 1993, 1994, 1995, 1996, 2000, 2001, 2002. Used by permission of NavPress Publishing Group.

All rights reserved. This book or any portion thereof may not be reproduced or used in any manner whatsoever without the express written permission of the publisher except for the use of brief quotations in a book review or scholarly journal.

First Printing: 2015

ISBN-13: 978-0692387160
ISBN-10: 0692387161

Cornelius Dixon Ministries
38 Southpointe Drive
Luverne, Alabama 36049
www.facebook.com/Kingdom.Mandate.Outreach.Ministries

Dedication

I dedicate this book to a very special young lady in our community. Breonia N. Parks. Battling Cancer at age 16, her faith and trust in God to help her and bring her through is true example of holding on, when the odds are stacked against you. Bre I want you to know we all are praying for you and your family! We love you and we continue to stand by your side! You have been a great inspiration to your family, friends, church, and community!

Unfortunately, Breonia passed away before the release of this book; but we honor her memories. So we say Rest in peace Breonia, until we see you again!

I also dedicate this work to my Aunt, Mary Dixon. Auntie you have been one of the greatest sources of support, encouragement, and correction. You have kept me focused and made sure I didn't give up when times got rough. You stood by my side and you never went behind my back and I thank God for you. Even in your battle with cancer, you kept the faith, and you continued to strive to do everything you can. I thank God he has healed you and that you are still here. I just want you to know I love you and I can never repay you for all the love you have given to me.

Table of Contents

Acknowledgments	ix
Foreword	xi
Preface	xv
Introduction	xix
Chapter 1: Embracing your life	1
Chapter 2: Understanding your rope	6
Chapter 3: The Spirit	8
Chapter 4: Faith	20
Chapter 5: Attitude is everything	28
Chapter 6: Model Prayer Outline	32
Chapter 7: What is your rope connected too?	37
Chapter 8: There's a Reason behind the madness	40
Chapter 9: Dangerous Conditions to your rope	43
Chapter 10: The power within your reach	55
Chapter 11: My Struggles, My Failures, My Victories	58
Chapter 12: Hang on in there!	64
Chapter 13: The Conclusion	67
Chapter 14: You will survive on purpose	69
Word from the Author	77
About The Author	79

Acknowledgments

First I would like to thank God, for just being GOD. Without him, and all the love he has for me; this project would not have been a success. So happy to serve the one and true God!

I would like to thank my Pastor and Elect Lady S.L. & Tanya Lowery & the St. James Missionary Baptist Church (Rutledge Alabama), thank you for standing by my side, and seeing the greatness in me, even when I couldn't see it in myself.; for all of the support, encouragement, correction and love that you and the family show me.

I would like to thank My "Mommy" Devona & Fredrick Jones, and Mya Harris. You have shown so much love and support. Thank you for all that you have done! I love you!

I would like to Thank Sheila and Myesha Foster for all the love you've shown.

I would like to thank Michelle, Marquitra, and Makiya Smith you stood by me in one of the hardest situations of my life, you didn't judge me, but gave me a shoulder to cry on and a place to lay my head. I can never forget what you have done!

I would like to thank Latrece Hall for all your encouragement and help through this writing process. Keeping me centered, and helping me believe in myself. And loving me unconditionally.

To Pastor James & Kawannon Taylor, thank you for standing in the gap and being a help to me in my growth. I look forward to more fellowship in this year and years to come!

Foreword

Cornelius W. Dixon is a young and empowering man of God who reveals his love for God by serving others and proclaiming the word of God through inspiring teaching and preaching. In this book, he shares his deepest thoughts and reveals his passion for a more meaningful life with God. It is Cornelius's hope that as he speaks from his heart others will draw closer to Christ and too seek to live a more fulfilling life. Minister Dixon's life journey has been a testimony of personalized faith that has strengthened his character and allowed him to be a proactive servant in the Christian Community. Although God is not finished with him yet, he is a positive force in the ministry that all can come to know and respect what God has entrusted in his hands.

Kawannon Taylor, M.S.

"Therefore, my beloved brethren, be steadfast, immovable, always abounding in the work of the Lord, knowing that your labor is not in vain."
1 Corinthians 15:58

Preface

How many times have you faced situations in life, and you seem to have tried any and everything to get out but nothing works. You pray, and pray, and pray; yet it seems as if the praying goes no further than the ceiling. We begin to question God and question ourselves in hopes to find an answer as to why this situation is occurring in our lives. We ask a question "How did I let it get like this?" Lately I have found myself asking that question in multiple areas of my life. As a result I found that in every area, the situation always came back to Obedience and the lack thereof. You know those habits we have, and we seem to lose focus on how God wants us to do things. God continuously warns us to stop, and a lot of times we fail to adhere to the voice of God. He continues to prompt us to prayer, but we find so many other things to do, and we say I will pray later. He makes so many appeals to us, and we never realize that we have rejected him in our everyday lives. It is at that moment, when God tries another approach to get your attention. He allows the conditions of life to change and we now face storms of life that begins to beat on us, and it seems like all hope is now gone. We then in a state of devastation and desperation remember the God of Israel, whom we have rejected throughout our days.

I found myself in this situation. As I sit here, a licensed minister of Christ; locked up in the Crenshaw County Jail. I began to ask those questions; why? How? How long? And the fact I wanted to blame others who had taken part, yet; I couldn't deny the fact that it was still my fault. How? Because God had been ministering to me and trying to tell me things but, I allowed my agenda and my desires to take presidency over God's plan. I was rejecting him; unintentionally, yet rejected none the less. When I woke up I failed to at least say thank you. When I drove my car up and down the streets, came close to wrecking at times yet, I failed to say thank you. I was so concerned about my outside Christianity that I failed to maintain my internal relationship with Christ. Now I was forced into the position to where I had no other choice but to look to God. I began praying, and most importantly examined MYSELF and began to repent; because I needed to hear from God and fast!

The Scripture Came to mind, Haggai 1:7"...*Consider your ways!*" I had to look back and reflect on life and I had to acknowledge that I never handled a lot of situations the right way. God had been appealing for me to pray more, fast more, and study more; but yet I found other things to do. So an old loan that I had not paid back caught up with me and landed me in jail. Then the Lord spoke to me and said, "Now that Facebook is out of the way, now that all of these women you text and call more than you talk to me, now that all of these distractions are no longer available to you; will you listen to me? Will you talk to me?" As tears rolled down my face; I laid back on the bed, and as I looked to the ceiling there was a poster glued to the light cover. It showed a picture of Jesus with his arms open wide, The caption above said "My job is to give you life, and that in its fullness." with the scripture "For I know the thoughts I think toward you, says the Lord, Thoughts of peace and not of evil to bring you to a future and a hope.'.

I knew then that God yet loved me in spite of my ignorance, and I was able to identify why these situations continued to occur in my life. As God ministered to me, I began to write just to clear my head. I remembered hearing in church "When your ropes seem to keep on breaking sometime; JUST REACH UP!" So when your rope keeps on breaking, you have to reach beyond the break. I was now in transition, and one of the most powerful things that really gave me the passion to hold on is; the text message I received from Elect Lady Tan, before I was taken in the jail house; it said "Dixon, you have to trust God even when the odds are stacked against you." God has a way of bringing you to reality. When he speaks, you have to listen!

No matter what it is that you may be facing. When your ropes seems to be breaking, just remember that there is power in Reaching beyond the break. Trust God, even when the odds are stacked against you. Knowing that the God we serve, if we yield our entire being to him, he will cause all things to work out in our favor. For it is in him that we live, move, and have our being.

Introduction

In this book we discuss the analogy of "the rope"; as well as its relevance to the lives we live, the making, the connection, the breaking points, the reason to reach beyond those breaks, and possible reasons as to why things are happening in our lives.

Zerubbabel and the people of Israel, had been enduring 70 years of Babylonian captivity because, they failed to adhere to the warnings that the prophets of God had been bringing too them. They were living a life that was not pleasing to God, continuously rejecting him, the words he send and the messengers he sent to them. God then allowed them to be taken over by the Babylonian government. The Babylonians came in and killed every man, woman, boy and girl; and began to take things of value from the house of God. They also destroyed the city and tore down its walls, burned down the houses and destroyed the house of the Lord. The bible records that the people who had escaped the massacre, was taken to Babylon as slaves. They were to endure this exile for 70 years, and at the end of those seventy years, they were released; and allowed to come back to Jerusalem to live there. It is here, that they were allowed back into the promise of God that he had promised to their forefathers. The bible says that they came together and decided to rebuild the city, and to rebuild the house of God; but before they did anything else, they were wise enough to restore worship; then they began to rebuild the temple (Ezra Chapter 1-3).

Now here is where our story of reaching beyond the break takes place. As the people began to rebuild the house of God, they ran into "Haters" that resisted them, in rebuilding the temple. Ezra 4:1 *"Now when the adversaries of Judah..."* The adversaries of Judah, which is translated to mean praise, they heard about the people who were once in exile; are now back in the city and are in the process of rebuilding the temple. They make up in their minds to disguise themselves as people wanting to help, but all the while they were against the move of God. They had a hidden agenda. Ultimately they wanted to stop the move and got the king to make a decree that the reconstruction must stop. Now Zerubbabel here is discouraged, and God see's his despair. God sent to him a Prophet by the name of Zechariah to give him a word to let him know that the reconstruction of the temple will happen, and he said that it's **"not by might, nor by power, but by my spirit; says the Lord."** (Zech. 4:6).

He was in a place where he had to learn to reach beyond the break and hold on until God made a way for him. Not by might denotes that the physical strength of man is not going to be able to do it. Nor by power denotes that not even the physical power of man, such as job, degrees, positions are not going to be a part of it; but he assures them that it will happen BY HIS SPIRIT. Just know that your deliverance will come, you just have to reach beyond the break. Just like you, when you find yourselves trying to work your way up after you've experienced the breaking or falling in life, you have those people who appear to be with you, but, they are really against you in your recovery. Don't get discouraged!

CHAPTER 1

Embracing your life

"So God created man in his own image; in the image of God he created him; male and female he created them." Genesis 1:27

If I were to ask you the question, "who are you?" What would be your response? Who you are surpasses your name, race, religious status, and personality; those sorts of things. Who you are describes your life, your abilities both natural and supernatural; it acknowledges the essence of your being. Who you are in fullness, is who God has created you to be. It is my belief; that if we can embrace who we are, then we can embrace the life that comes with who we are. There is always a process that we go through, to reach our full potential in the life that God has for us, and because he knows us, we are able to make it through whatever we face in the life we are called to live. It is imperative for you to understand that "LIFE" will not always be easy; especially living the life of Holiness. Though it may be hard, temptation may be on every hand; trust God! Why? Because, there is a lesson to be learned. An anointing to obtain. You have to be able to accept the life you have, even when others may not seem to understand, GOD DOES!

Jeremiah 1:5, God explains to Jeremiah that way before he was conceived, God already knew who he wanted Jeremiah to be and what he wanted him to do. Before he came from his mother's womb God had already sanctified him to be that person he wanted him to be. God has a plan for your life, and created you to withstand the storm in order to get to that place. Jeremiah was his name, but a Prophet of God is who he was. Just like Jeremiah we all have our excuses as to why we are not qualified in our own eyes, but God knows it all, and he is there to guide us through the storms. You will encounter situations that may seem to utterly destroy you; but in reality, it is designed to give you tools that are needed to live as you have been ordained to live until Jesus Christ returns. It is at those times in our lives when we have to trust God even the more. Knowing that he holds true to his word; that He will never leave nor forsake you He will always be there.

We hear in church all the time "What don't kill you will only make you stronger", this saying is true: but, understand this vital key, it is not the intensity of the storm that determines your strength, however, it is the attitude you have and the ability to stand in the midst of opposition in your life. Will you allow the storms of life to cause you to run or give up at the first sign of adversity? Don't allow your current situations to make you run from God; allow it to draw you closer to him. Instead of making Permanent decisions for temporary situations, God wants us to give him a permanent praise in our temporary situations. James said count it all Joy when you face trials in life. 2Cor. 4:17 says *"for your light afflictions are only temporal, but is working for you a more precious and eternal weight of glory. (NKJV)"* It may not feel good right now, it may not look good or sound good, but its working for your good! There is something being created behind the scene that will benefit you for the long run. This is just an avenue you have to travel in your life to get to your destiny.

Know this, trial comes into your life under three categories. God testing, the devil tempting, and the desires your own flesh. These three together comes to teach you, correct you and form you in life. Let's look at these a little more before we get into the analogy of the "rope" and reaching beyond the break. Understand that God is not evil, so he therefore does not tempt us with evil, but, he tests us in those times to see if we will trust him; and keep pushing until we get to the place of promise. When God delivered the children of Israel he tested them by way of the wilderness. He intended to take them through a route that was suppose to take about two weeks to get through; but, because of their response to the hardship of the wilderness way, it took them forty years to come through. They mummer, they complained, they lashed out at the man of God. They were delivered physically but remained mentally bound. A lot of times we find ourselves being delivered yet bound; thus causing us to fail the test of time simply because our attitude is not right. Do not find yourselves in this place in your season of testing. It may cause you to stay longer than intended.

The devil comes into our lives at our weakest moments, to tempt and try and shake our faith. He knows the buttons to push in your life to try to knock you off course. At the time where the sons of God came to be in the presence of God the bible says Satan came along with them. God asked him, "Where are you coming from Satan?" Satan reply was, "from going to and fro, up and down the earth seeking whom I may devour." Satan has been watching you and he has his demons on dispatch to tempt you on every hand to curse God. God allows the tempting, but Satan has to have permission. He is allowed to tempt you with the lust of the flesh, the lust of the eyes, and the pride of life, but he is not allowed to touch your life. Thing I love about this story in Job, is the fact that he had enough faith in God; to wait on God to restore him. Job is a great example; he was a great and perfect Godly man, and though tragedy struck and he lost everything he had, He was able to keep a firm grip on life, holding on trusting God; in hopes that someday whether on earth or in heaven that he would gain what he lost. He said Naked I came, Naked I shall leave. For the Lord gives and the Lord have taken away. There are forty-two chapters in Job. From chapter one to chapter forty-one Job was experiencing trials and tribulation but in chapter forty-two Job was blessed with double. Now I don't know what chapter you are on in your life, but you just have to hold on, because there will come a "Job Forty-Two" in your life. Rejoice even more in the fact that after every chapter of your life there is a period, meaning that when God finishes there is nothing able to be added or taken away. Can you wait on God, even when it seems like everything around you is falling apart?

As human, we must be careful to control our flesh. Flesh will get us in trouble every time. A lot of times we are the very cause of things not working right in our lives because of our desires that we do not submit to the power of God. The bible teaches us that desire start in the heart, and if they are not dealt with, then they conceive actions in our mind; and further that conception births sin in our lives. We can only go so long until the world as we know it begins to crashing down around us. A pastor I sat under for a few years taught me a lesson that stuck with me; He said, SIN will do three things, Make you stay longer than you are willing to stay, Pay more than you're willing to pay, and do more than you're willing to do.

So in order for us to truly embrace this life, we have to crucify our flesh daily. Laying aside every weight and sin that doth so easily hinder us and run the race with patience! We all endure testing, for if we are not tested then how can we graduate to the next level? The sin is not being tested, but giving up and failing to trust God in the midst of the testing is the sin. We are all tempted in some way or another in our lives, but the sin is not the temptation, its yielding to the temptation. We are human, and our flesh desires things opposite to the spirit. The sin of it is the fact that we give into the flesh, and not allow the spirit to take control. Know that when you fall into sin, as my pastor teaches us, "When you mess up, 'Fess' up". We have an advocate with the father who is the propitiation for our sins. God forgives us and gives us a new chance. Embrace the life, and watch God show up mightily on your behalf. So as the prophet Haggai talks about, when things go wrong, before making excuses and trying to point the blame "Consider your ways". There is a reason behind the madness. Take just a few moments to pray this prayer, because, God wants to forgive you and I believe that if you sincerely say this prayer from your heart, that grace and mercy will stand up on your behalf, and God is saying to you today. No matter what you have done and no matter what you're going through right now; CASE DISMISSED!

Father, in Jesus name! Thank you; for your love and compassion being renewed daily for me. Thank you that even in my unfaithfulness; you've yet remained faithful to me. You didn't give up on me, even when I gave up on myself. God I ask that you will forgive me of every sin, every evil thought, and every sinful desire of my heart. Cleanse me, and bring me into right standing with you. I believe in your son, Jesus, and I thank you for the sacrifice he made for my sin. Wash me in the blood he shed, in Jesus name; AMEN.

CHAPTER 2

Understanding your rope

"For I know the thoughts that I think toward you, saith the Lord, thoughts peace and not of evil, to give you an expected end." Jeremiah 29:11

When your rope seems to keep on breaking, you have to reach up higher; and hold on. This saying seems easier said than done a lot of times. In holding on to the rope you must realize what your rope is. Your rope symbolizes the hope of your life in its fullness. It is holding on to the hopes, the dreams, the callings of life; it is the very life line of your destiny; it is in fact your life. What materials does your rope (life) consist of that will aide you in your holding on; until you reach the place of destiny that God has for your life? God created you for a specific purpose, for a specific time in a specific position; just like a rope. What do I mean? Ropes are designed to hold a certain amount of weight, in a certain position for a specific amount of time. It is the materials that the rope is made of that gives it the strength that it needs to support what its holding.

A rope is made up of fibers of thread twisted together with other fibers until it forms a strand, that strand is then twisted or braided with other strands until it forms the rope as we see it. Let's break that down just a little. The word fiber is described as being "Internal strength and Character", what is the internal strength or character of your rope? The internal strength and character of your rope is important, because if it's not built up the right material, then it will fail you when conditions surrounding it seem to pose a threat to it. This is why you find people killing themselves and giving up in every aspect of life. They've reached the breaking point and it caused them to want to give up. Remember when God told Noah to build the ark in preparation of the flood? Notice that when he gave him the assignment, He told him exactly what to build it with and exactly how to build. Why? Simply because, he needed the ark to be able to withstand against the beating of the storm. Just like the ark, your rope must be built for the storm.

The internal strength of the rope is the ability of the rope. It is the power of the rope. What does your life consist of to give you the necessary strength needed to make it in life no matter the condition. The internal strength then produces the character of the rope. The way it presents its self in the conditions of life weather good or bad. It determines how it acts. As I thought on this, I began to notice that; strength of the rope is the fibers, the character of the rope is the strand, and life is the rope.

If you have ever taken a rope apart, you find that it is made up of three or more strands; depending on the type of rope you have. As I've said the fibers represent the internal strength, which ultimately produces the strands; which represents the character of the rope. We are going to focus on a three strand rope in the following chapters.

CHAPTER 3

The Spirit

"But the fruits of the spirit is love, joy, peace, long-suffering, kindness, goodness, faithfulness, gentleness, self-control" Galatians 5:22-23

This talks about the benefit of walking/living in the spirit. It produces fruit that are nourishing to your rope. It is a character that births not only good actions, and sound attitudes but also divine strength.

What is the operation of the spirit in your rope? The spirit comes to do multiple things in the lives of the believers. The older saints always said the spirit is a keeper; he is a helper and a comforter. It gives encouragement and help when the conditions of life seem to become treacherous. The spirit will lead and guide you into all truths. I assure you that there will be seasons in your life where you just want to throw in the towel, but the spirit quickens you and gives you that extra push to keep pressing; no matter what comes your way. Just like the story explained in the introduction, about Zerubbabel. Only way you can survive and make it is by Gods spirit. The spirit within us is that divine force that gives us life, power, and strength. Without the spirit of God we are worthless, we are nothing, and can do nothing without God. When holding on, we must allow God to put his super with our natural. It is only by his spirit, are we made alive, energetic, and powerful.

When the spirit is involved; he does the work, you just have to hold on. Philippians 1:6 says, **"Being confident of this very thing, that he who has begun a good work in you will complete it until the day of Jesus Christ;"** If we walk in the spirit, we then have it working on the inside of us. In spite of your current situation; the spirit is always at work. It does not resign at the sign of hardship, but rather it continues to work. This is why the spirit is a vital strand to our lives, because it gives us life, not just in a respiratory perspective but in a mobility perspective as well. Think of Ezekiel in the valley of the dry bones, even after he prophesied and all the bones and flesh came into its respective places, the bible said that he looked out among them and there was still no life. It wasn't until he prophesied and commanded the four winds and the breath of life to come forth and breathe life into those that were slained; that they were able to stand as an exceedingly great army. Then God said something so powerful at the conclusion of that text. He said in a nut shell, "I will give you hope, I will give you life, and place you in the land of promise. They shall know that, He is the Lord and He has spoken and performed it." Your hardship may have been a result of some behavior on your behalf, but when the spirit of God comes in it gives you hope, life, and restore you in the place of promise. Then will know who God is. So what then are the fibers that manifest the strand of the spirit, or that identifies that the spirit is in operation in your life? Galatians 5:22-23 notifies them as ***"The fruits of the spirit"***. I remind you that the strands of the rope, represents the character and/or behavior of your rope. And the Fiber represents the internal strength of your rope. So let's take a moment to deal with these nine "*fibers*" individually.

Love:
"And now abide faith, hope, love these three; but the greatest of these is love." 1 Corinthians 13:13

Love in this text is shown as a motivation or strength. It is a reason to do what you do, in hopes of being an instrument of God. Love is defined as an expression of intense affection that arises out of kinship from personal ties; it is being fond of another. See when you have love, you do things for the right reasons. Love is one of the most important fibers of our ropes, because without love, all we say and do becomes empty and void. It has no structure, no commitment, and no substance; it fails easily because there is no character without love. Love in this text goes beyond being an expression or an emotion, it is a character. Emotions and expressions can often times change due to the current conditions, but real love never waivers. I don't care how saved you think you are, or how successful you think you've been, you can have more degrees than a thermometer but if you don't have love in your heart; you're just making noise. We need Love in our hearts. Because with love, you can treat your neighbor right, even when they do you wrong. With love you don't have room to hate, or hate on anyone because of their current status in life. Preachers I don't care how well you preach. I don't care how well you pray, without love; you're just putting on a show. Saints I don't care how much faith you have operating in your life, without love you still live defeated. Whatever you say or whatever you do, if you don't have love; you will profit nothing. When you love like God says love, no matter what your enemies throw your way, you are able to love them. That's the kind of love that Jesus had for us! The bible says, while we were yet in our sins Christ died, furthermore and rose again. He endured the pressures of life for us, he gave up his life for us, and, he went through persecution and beatings so that we may live.

Joy:
"then he said to them, 'go your way, eat the fat, drink the sweet, and send portions to those whom nothing is prepared; for this day is a holy day to our Lord. Do not sorrow, for the joy of the Lord is your strength."
Nehemiah 8:10

Joy, like love is a fiber of rope that you cannot afford to live without. It is another manifestation of spiritual strength. Without joy, you very well may not have the physical or mental capacity to deal with the obligations that come with the various seasons of your life, in every aspect of life. Joy is defined to be in a place much deeper than contentment, and more powerful than happiness. It is a place of divine satisfaction. People and things in your life can make you happy, but only God can give you Joy. Joy is like an anointing; it can only flow from the top down. It cannot be imitated, It cannot be duplicated, It cannot be bought, it cannot be borrowed; you have to birth this thing. When you obtain joy in your life, you not only gain the needed strength; but, also healing to the wounded or broken areas of your life. Proverbs 22:7 says *"A merry heart does the body good like a medicine, but, a broken spirit rotten the bones"* Joy is the cure for the brokenness of your spirit. It brings you into a place of divine spiritual healing. That's why the bible says in Isaiah 61:3 *"... To give beauty for ashes, the oil of joy for morning, the garment of praise for the spirit of heaviness..."* Joy operates in every circumstance of life that you encounter. It is our way of escape from the pressure of life. That's why you will hear people saying, "I don't look like what I've been through" because Joy totally shields you from the pressures of hardship. Joy is something you need. I never really understood the saying, "out of all that I've been through, I still have joy"; until I experienced the power of Joy for myself. Because no matter what circumstance may come, I remain joyful in God because of who he is and what he is able to do in my situation. Even though I may get hit, but I still have joy. Though it may seem as if things are going terrible, I still have joy' because the God I serve is able to handle my every situation. Even in this season of your life, you may have to bend but Joy will keep you from breaking. You may have to cry sometime but the word says that weeping may endure for the night but, joy will come in the morning. Don't allow anything to hinder the joy of the Lord from operating in your life. My grandmother said "This joy that I have, the world didn't give it to me and the world can't take it away" how do you protect the joy you have? By putting on the garment of praise that God may be glorified in your situation!

So no matter what you may be facing right now, if you have the spirit of the living God down on the inside, you then have his joy. If you have Joy, then you have supernatural strength, and if you have strength you have the ability to handle the obligations that are required of you in this season of your life. That's why in Nehemiah 8, when the law was read and the people became overwhelmed and they began to weep. Nehemiah told them "go your way, eat and drink, give unto those who nothing is prepared for this day is holy unto the Lord. Do not sorrow, for the Joy of the Lord is your strength." it may be dark in your life right now, but the darkest part of the night is right before the breaking of day. Just hang on in there, knowing that God will deliver you on time!

Peace:
"These things I have spoken to you, that in me you might have peace. In the world you will have tribulation; but be of good cheer, I have overcome the world." John 16:33

Jesus lets us know here that only way we find peace in a world of tribulation is in him. Because of his sacrifice for our sins. The shedding of his blood and him rising again; brought us into a covenant of peace if we receive him. Peace is defined as a state of tranquility and calm. It's an expression of serenity; by changing the things you can, and allowing God to handle the things you cannot change. Not being easily burden by the pressures of life; peace makes it easy to go through. Remember the story in the bible, when Jesus and the twelve disciples were crossing the sea, and there came a great storm? Out of fear the disciples began to cry out to God, Jesus arose and said "Peace; be still" and the wind and sea calmed. You have to know how to speak peace over your situations. Without peace fear begins to set in and intimidate you and cause you to panic, even when Jesus is right there in your face. When you have peace in your life, though the world may be falling all around you, you remain faithful in God and not allow the conditions of your surroundings to hinder you from living and pressing toward that life that you desire to live. Peace is an important characteristic; peace comes as a mindset in the midst of turbulence. When peace is an attribute of your life, then you are able to hold your peace when opposition comes your way. No matter what comes your way and no matter how long you have to endure it, you can make it. No matter the tribulations of the world. You can have peace because Jesus has already overcome the world on our behalf, All we have to do is go through; but you have to have the right mindset. Romans 8:6 says *"for to be carnally minded is death, but to be spiritually minded is life and peace"* Don't allow the mindset of the world to pattern your life or thoughts. Only way you can have a spiritual mind, is if you present your body a living sacrifice, holy and acceptable unto God. Not being conformed to the world but being transformed by the renewing of our minds, and then the peace of God which surpasses all understanding will guard your heart and minds. It's all in the mind. The mind is a terrible thing to lose, live in peace and don't allow the conditions of your life to make you lose your mind.

When you have the love of God in your heart. The Joy of the Lord in your spirit. The peace of God in your mind. Then the next fiber of your rope almost comes easy.

Long-suffering:
"Wherefore seeing we also are compassed about with so great a cloud of witnesses, let us lay aside every weight and the sin which doth so easily beset us, and let us run with patience the race that is set before us," Hebrews 12:1 (KJV)

A lot of times we see this word, and ultimately want to give up. People want the glory in a situation but never want to go through it. To have long suffering means to suffer long, to be patient and endure the situation until the process is complete. It is to, not give up so easily; but to hold on no matter how long the situation, knowing God will strengthen you. God is long-suffering with us, and so we should be long-suffering with ourselves and each other. No matter what it looks like, no matter how it feels, we should be able to stand until God comes in our behalf.

Many times in life you will find that your desires in life will often time come with a test, or a seasonal process to test and prepare you for the things that is to come; later in your life. You have to be willing to endure the process in order to make it through it and become that person that you desire and, furthermore you have to endure in order to become that person that God has ordained you to be. So that at the time of birthing; beholding the glory that was once considered an affliction is much more special and appreciated. Don't give up! Hebrews 12 says that you should "lay aside every weight and sin that easily beset (to ensnare, hinder, or prolong) us" a lot of times we take on so much from the world; that it makes it hard for us to endure the race. It's hard to run a marathon with ankle weights and shackles on your feet. That represents the mental burdens and sinful attire that we wear. We have to separate ourselves from those things in order to run with endurance, and overcome the obstacles that we may face. Looking unto Jesus, who is with us along the way and also stands at the finished line with a reward in his hands waiting to tell us WELL DONE! So no matter how long your tracks keep running, no matter the obstacles that have been placed in your way keep running. It's not about trying to outdo anyone, or rushing to get done because Ecclesiastes 9:11 says *"... The race is not given to the swift, nor the battle to the strong, nor bread to the wise, nor riches to the men of understanding, nor favor to the men of skill; but time and chance happen to them all."* There is and appointed time of deliverance for you, you just have to endure the trial. You may not be the fastest one, you may not be the strongest, or the wisest the most wealthy; all that has nothing to do with your deliverance. Whoever you are, and whatever your current status in life; just know that there is an appointed time just for you. The text says time and chance happens to them all, you just have to stay in the race! I wrote a song called, He'll see you through. It talks about running in the race no matter the obstacles to come. Regardless what happens, you have to keep on running in the race, and keep on fighting until you see his face, keep on pressing and God will make a way for you. Just put your trust in Jesus I know He'll see you through. You may get tired along the way but hold your head up and keep the faith. Put all of your trust Jesus for God will see you through.

Gentleness:
"Let your gentleness be known to all men. The Lord is at hand."
Philippians 4:5

Gentleness is to be refined and well mannered. To be easily handled and managed. It is to be humble. Too many times when we go through a situation we wear our feelings on our sleeves. We become moody, hard to minister too, and corrected in some situations. When we humble ourselves and allow God to do his work in us; then we are able to hold on to our ropes of life in the midst of the storms. 1Peter 5:5 teaches to be *"clothe in humility because God resists the proud and gives grace to the humble."* When we humble ourselves, God gives us grace to aid us in the process. Humility is needed because, pride will destroy us. We are to be as fierce as a lion but, as humble as a dove. Know that God is watching us. Philippians says all men should be able to see our gentleness, because, in seeing the gentleness in us; others may be drawn to Christ. We ought to be so humble that when people see us, they see the Jesus in us. Jesus is coming back really soon, and we shouldn't be found pushing people away, but drawing them closer with the spirit of humility. You are not the only one going through!

Goodness:
"Therefore consider the goodness and severity of God: on those who fell, severity; but toward you, goodness, if you continue in his goodness. Otherwise you also will be cut off." Romans 11:22

Goodness is having a favorable quality; Being morally excellent. When our lifestyles are in good nature, we then become partakers in the goodness of Christ. God's blessings and grace reigns on the just as well as the unjust; but his favor, is only prepared for those who are in position to receive it. Paul told Titus in Chapter 3, to teach the elders to live their lives in a way that shows their dedication and commitment to God. Not to be gossips or drunks, but to be examples of goodness. We need to live by example. We ought to show off the goodness of God through our living. According to Romans 11:22, if you do not continue in goodness and virtue; you will be cut off. Like those who decided to operate outside of the integrity and virtue that we are called too. Integrity will take you a long way in life. Integrity will make you do the right thing even when no one is watching. When you allow God's goodness to overtake you, and operate in that goodness then, when you walk through valley of the shadow of death there is no reason to fear anything evil because God is with you! Surely goodness and mercy is following behind you; keeping the mistakes from the past from taking aim at you.

Faith:
"Behold the proud, his soul is not upright in him; but the just shall live by his faith." Habakkuk 2:4

We know that the only way to please God in life is to live according to faith. Faith is a very powerful fiber and very important. The attitude of faith says, "even though I can't see it, I know it's there. Though it may not seem possible I know it's coming." Jesus said, that if you have faith as a grain of a mustard seed, you can move all mountains. It is not speaking of the size, but rather the power that abides in the seed. Being that it's so small, yet, produces greater sized harvest. Faith will cause you to praise God in the midst of a breaking situation. I love the story of Jehoshaphat going into battle. When he heard that a great multitude had assembled together to fight against him, and the people of Judah and Jerusalem. The bible says Jehoshaphat began to fear. Here is where faith kicked in, right after fear manifested Jehoshaphat, (according to 2 Chronicles 20) set himself or, positioned himself to seek the Lord! He and the inhabitants began to praise God. Faith will help you to position yourself to trust God even when it seems as if you cannot trace him. As a result of their faithful seeking, the spirit of the Lord came in and said to them "Listen, do not be afraid of this great multitude that is coming up against you." faith tells you listen, you don't have to fear what it looks like; because the battle is not yours it belongs to God. He said don't be afraid or dismayed because of what you are going through. That word dismayed means "to be made unable". Fear will cripple your ability to believe and therefore cause you to walk in doubt; and if you are in doubt, you can't experience the victory that God has already given you. So don't allow your situation to come in and make you doubt God. So he told them "Tomorrow go to the battle, for the Lord is with you. Even though it may seem big, even though it may seem like you can't handle it, even though it may seem like you can't make it through don't fear what it looks like; just go through it. It may seem hard in your life right now, just go through it. All hell may be breaking loose around you, just go through it. My favorite part of that text is when they went down to the battle, Jehoshaphat sent out the praise and worshiper before he sent out the army. Your faith and praise is the best weapons to use in the battle. God reigned in victory in that situation. I encourage you, no matter what the equation is, know that faith is always the answer to the problem. For we walk by faith, and not by sight.

You can make it to that life you dream of. Though the vision is just for an appointed time, in faith and believing that "God Will"; wait for it. Though it may tarry, wait for it because it shall surely come, and will not tarry. No matter how hard it gets, keep the faith Paul said "Above all taking up the shield of faith, that you may be able to quench the fiery darts of the wicked one." Faith is the key to unlocking the things God has for you. When you have dreams in life, faith will aide you in those things coming to pass. Faith helps the outcome of your situation. Without faith, the woman with the issue of blood would not be made whole; but, her faith was stronger than her fear. When you allow faith to take precedence over fear, the things you face will not be a hindrance; but it will be a stepping stone. Don't allow fear to take the place of faith in your life. When fear comes, rebuke it in prayer; and watch God work. Use your trial to exercise your faith. Faith without works is dead.

Meekness:
"Therefore lay aside all filthiness and overflow of wickedness, and receive with meekness the implanted word, which is able to save your souls." James 1:21

This is an area that most of us have a problem in. To show meekness is to be submissive. We have a problem with that in many ways, and thus causes situations of life be worse than normal. We have to learn the importance of submission, however, that does not mean letting people run over you. It is to submit yourself to the presiding Authority. When we learn to submit to authority, many of the battles we fight would not even be an issue. The focal point of this particular message though is to submit to the authority of God and to be gentle toward all men. If you are submitted to God; when things come your way, you speak in his name and what you are facing has to fall in submission. Here it is our foundation. The scripture says, to lay aside all the sin and wickedness and receive with Meekness the implanted word; which is able to save your soul. In receiving and submitting yourself to God's word, you then become saved and healed; and partakers of all the promises of God concerning you, as the elect of God. Receive with meekness the implanted word of God. The things he speaks into your spirit through his messengers, through his word, and through prayer. Whether they are encouraging or rebuking, receive with meekness the Words of the Lord. Matthew 5:2 says *"Blessed are the meek, for they shall inherit the earth"* the meek are a happy people. Who find themselves in a place of undisturbed enjoyment with life, friends, and God; even in the midst of trouble! For they shall inherit the land; not always meaning materialistic but spiritually. Just as the land of Canaan was perceived as a land like heaven, so it is here in this text. We find a place of heaven on earth in the spirit of meekness. The meek will rather forgive 100 injuries; than to take revenge on one. The meek are fit for life and ready for death; because, they have their hearts fixed and minds made up to live by the spirit.

Temperance:
"Do you not know that those who run in a race all run, but one receives the prize? Run in such a way that you may obtain it. And everyone who competes for the prize is temperate in all things. Now they do it to obtain a perishable crown, but we for an imperishable crown." 1Corinthians 9:24-25

I have three words for this fiber, "Keep your cool." In life you will find that self-control is a very important fiber to have. With self control we find those angry moments ultimately pacified, and not find ourselves acting out. In life you will face moments that call for temperance. It is with temperance, that we are able to roll with the punches until we reach our blessed place. A lot of times you find things not working out for your good; because, as human we have the tendency to "fly off the handles" when we face difficult times. Self-control helps you to deal with them and not lose your composure; so that you can hold on in the midst of opposition.

It is important to have these fruits of the spirit, Galatians said in chapter 5 verse 23-24 "...Against such there is no law. And those who are in Christ have crucified the flesh with its passions and its desire." In order for these fibers to begin to operate in your life, you have to first of all crucify the flesh. You cannot experience the benefits of the spirit while fulfilling the lust of the flesh. The flesh will make you do the complete opposite of what the spirit wills for you to do. Don't let the flesh hinder you from living as the spiritual being you were designed to live.

CHAPTER 4

Faith

"But also for this very reason, giving all diligence, add to your faith virtue, to virtue knowledge, to knowledge self control, to self control perseverance, to perseverance godliness, to godliness brotherly kindness, and to brotherly kindness love. For if these things are yours and abound, you will be neither barren nor unfruitful in the knowledge of our Lord Jesus Christ." 2 Peter 1:5-8

The second strand of your rope should be faith. We have discussed "Faith" as fiber or strength. Now let's discuss faith as a Character of your rope. Faith is a very important strand, because, without faith it will be impossible for you to keep a good grasp on your rope. Having received faith is a great starting point; however, we should begin to grow in faith; by adding more fibers in it in order for us to become perfected. If we are to make any progress we must be diligent in all we do, because without giving all diligence; there is no gain in the life of holiness. Our lives as believers are made out step by step. The bible said that our steps have already been ordered, and walking in those steps cause us to obtain the strength needed to endure our storms. What are some of those strengths (Fibers)?

Virtue:
"Finally, brethren, whatever things are true, whatever things are noble, whatever things are just, whatever things are pure, whatever things are lovely, whatever things are of good report, If there be

any virtue, and if there is anything praiseworthy- meditate on these things." Philippians 4:8

By obtaining virtue, we will understand strength and power; without which, you will not be able to stand in good works. Refusing virtue will make you a "coward Christian". Causing you to be ashamed of your faith; when the times of trial come into your life. Being ashamed of your faith; will cause God to be ashamed of you before his father. We need virtue to live, and it will benefit us not only in life but death also. Virtue helps to heal our situation. When the woman with the issue of blood came to Jesus, in faith she spoke "If I could just touch his clothes then I will be made whole." and in the touch of faith; the virtue came from Jesus and immediately her affliction had been cured. When we operate in faith and allow the healing virtue in God to take effect in our lives; then the issues we face will all be cured. Now be careful to use the correct virtue in this, there are different types.

One type is called "Cardinal Virtue". Cardinal Virtue is those things that we consider to be important or a characteristic in virtue. Things like Justice, prudence, temperance and fortitude.

Another type is called "Natural Virtue". Natural virtue is those things man accomplishes without direct help from God. Such as Cardinal virtues; justice, prudence, temperance, and fortitude.

The last type is called "Theological Virtue". That is the characteristics placed in man by the special grace of God, like faith, hope, and love.

It shouldn't take rocket science to determine which one of these virtues would be beneficial to our ropes.

We cannot fully rely on the Cardinal and Natural virtues, because they are outside of God. The theological Virtues are the characteristics we need. We as saints must be careful to walk according to the spirit. Although we live in the flesh, we do not live according to the flesh. The bible teaches about the weapons in which we fight with are not carnal, but are mighty in God. We are not to live according to the flesh. How do we do this? By not being conformed to the philosophy or systems of the world. Instead, being transformed in the spirit of our minds, and presenting ourselves living sacrifices unto God.

Knowledge:
"The fear of the Lord is the beginning of knowledge, but fools despise wisdom and instruction." Proverbs 1:7

To virtue, Paul says too add knowledge. Knowledge is being familiar with, aware of, and/or understanding of particular a person, place, or thing. How can knowledge benefit our spiritual lives; and be strength of our spiritual ropes? Because, if we line our lives up in God's word he then gives us knowledge to understand the content of our situations; which differs according to the individual, and the degree in which it effects the persons mindset. It helps us to understand the importance or intensity of the situation; and the lessons to be learned through it. Knowledge is obtained through life's experiences or teachings. By the way we perceive, discover, and learn in life. Knowledge is key to us, because, without knowledge we perish. When you receive knowledge, what are you going to do with it? It is imperative that we incorporate knowledge into our lives and act on it.

Now Solomon says that the fear of the Lord is the starting point in the reception of knowledge. When we give Jesus our all, and allow him to live in us as we live for him; then we can obtain knowledge through him. There is absolutely no reason for us to ask God for knowledge if we are not going to put it to work. Your knowledge will help keep you grounded in faith. My grandmother always said "Baby when you know that you know, that you know that you know…" that simply means that when you face a "Breaking" moment, when you know, that you know, that you know; that GOD IS ABLE, then no matter the situation you are facing; you have the ability to hold on. Because, you know that God is coming to your rescue. Just as the three Hebrew boys faced with the fiery furnace, they could have gave in to the kings command to worship his image; but, they stood their ground; because of their knowledge of GOD and his word! When you have knowledge of the word and the promises that it gives to you; no matter the situations that come up in your life, you have the ability through the knowledge of the word to hold on. Such as, Isaiah 54:17 *"no weapon formed against you shall prosper..."* in the midst of adversity, you can hang on; because, the word has promised a solution to your situation, even before it began.

You may be wondering "How do I obtain this knowledge?" Psalms 1:2-3 declares, **"But** ***his delight is in the law of the Lord, and on His law does he meditate both day and night. And he shall be like a tree planted by the rivers of water, which brings forth fruit in its season and whose leaf shall not wither. And whatsoever he does shall prosper."*** Upon the reception of Jesus into your life, the next step is studying and applying his word in your life. That way when faced with situations of life, you have the word to help you. It is considered to be a principle to the promises. God's word not only gives knowledge, but, it gives you the power needed to strengthen your life. However, this doesn't mean trial won't come, because they surely will come; but it won't destroy you. Just remind yourself daily, that the people perish for the lack of knowledge.

Self-control:
"A person without self control is like a house with its doors and windows knocked out." Proverbs 25:28 (The Message)

The next fiber in our ropes is self control. Although self control is the same as temperance in our previous strand; it has a different function in this particular strand of our ropes. This function is keeping control over your spirit. By controlling what you allow to come in and/or be released. For example, let's look at the biblical principles of marriage. 1Corinthians 7 teaches about relationships, and how it's not good for a man to touch a woman and having only one spouse. Verse 5 talks about how the spouses should not keep each other from being pleased sexually. The only reason to deny your spouse sexual affection; is to give yourselves to fasting and prayer. Then coming back together, that "Satan does not tempt you for your lack of self-control". Simply put don't be so quick to jump into any and everything. Don't continue to put more on yourselves that in your lack of self control the enemy blinds you and then binds you. A lot of times we become burnt out because we lack self-control in the things we do. We begin to bite off more than we can chew. You have to remember that your rope is designed to endure certain conditions, and it's imperative that we not add more unnecessary weight to our ropes.

Solomon tells us in the text, that a man with the lack of self-control is compared to a city with no walls. Therefore leaving the city open and vulnerable for the enemy to come in, and sow seeds of discord, and cause chaos on those who dwell in that city. We cannot allow ourselves to be open to destruction. It's not only dangerous for the individual, but, for those who are connected to them as well. I remember a parable that Jesus was teaching on the "Wheat and Tares", how when the people slept and the enemy came in and sowed tares among the wheat to choke out, kill, and destroy it; Because the people were sleeping on their jobs the security of the land was breached, and the enemy crept in. Don't find yourself sleeping on your job. The enemy is walking among us, waiting for someone to devour. The enemy seeks to destroy you. Just as Jesus told peter; "Satan desires to sift you as wheat," but the prayer is that you remain faithful in all things. Believe this, Satan sits at the door; and waits for an opportune time to enter in and destroy what you are trying to accomplish. Do not give him the lead to come in and do anything that causes you to mess up the life you are destined to live. Of course he will tempt you, but you have the freedom of choice. Control yourselves through fasting, prayer, and meditation of God's word.

Patience:
"That you do not become sluggish, but imitate those who in faith and patience inherit the promises." Hebrews 6:12

Paul is teaching the people in Rome the gift of the testimony of the people who received the promises of God through faith and the perseverance through trials. Through faith and patience, denotes they had enough trust in God to continue to do the work of ministry; and knowing God would not ignore the labor they have done for his name sake, in the midst of their trials. That pushed them to wait for him to deliver them and reward them with the promises. We sometimes want to give up to quickly when it comes to waiting on God. In all that Job went through, he waited on God and God blessed him with a double portion. Waiting on God has its rewards all in itself. Hebrews 10:36 says, *"For you have need of endurance, so that **after** you have done the will of God, you may receive the promise."* Your waiting will not be in vain. Failure to wait on the promises of God hinders you from receiving the promises that God has for you. God does not now, never have, nor will he ever need your help bringing forth what he promised you; all he need you to do is wait patiently on him to move. Abraham was promised a son through his wife Sara, and because they were old, they figured they would help God by Abraham having a son with Sara's maid. Remember, when it comes to God working things in your life, your current condition is no problem for God. Just because it may look one way to you, we serve a God who is able to do what he needs to do. Though you may get what you was looking for, that does not fulfill God's promise and purpose for your life. Though they had Ishmael, Isaac was still the promise. You have need for endurance, though the vision may tarry, wait on it, for it shall surely come. They that wait on the Lord, has a renewed strength, the ability to soar above the storms, walk in peace and destiny, & run in purpose. You just have to live by faith!

Godliness:
"But reject profane and old wives' fables, and exercise yourself toward Godliness. For bodily exercise profits a little, but godliness is profitable for all things, having promise of the life that is now and of that which is to come." 1 Timothy 4:7, 8

Godliness is the practice of holy living in all areas of life; such as deeds, thoughts, conversation, etc. God's word tells us to be holy, for Christ is holy. Godliness is going further than having the Christian Character. It's not just a saying or a title; it is to be a lifestyle. Hebrews 12:14 says, **"Pursue peace with all men, and Holiness, without which no man shall see the Lord."** If

Godliness is not a part of our ropes, we are then help captive by the systems of the world. Godliness denotes your lifestyle beyond Sunday morning, after the music stops, after the benediction, after you've left from the presence of the fellow saints. Godliness is how you live behind closed doors. Godliness and Holiness is not hard to accomplish.

According to 2 Peter 1:3 ***"as His divine power has given us all things that pertain to life and godliness, through the knowledge of him who called us by glory and virtue."*** Through the knowledge of Christ in his word and by his divine power, we have all that we need to live life in holiness. For this reason Paul encourages Timothy to reject the Godless myths and old wives' tales and train yourselves to live holy. We cannot allow the secular mentality to govern our lives. The ways of the world is not the way of God. God's ways, gives blessings for the life we live now and the life that is to come in heaven. That's why he went on to say in 2 Timothy 4:8 that to exercise the physical body profits a little, but in exercising the spiritual body through Godliness, gives promise to the life that we live now and shall live later. Godliness brings about eternal blessings. God desires for us to live a peaceable lifestyle through Godliness and in reverence to Him. It should not be our focus to gain materialistic things, but to gain the blessings of spirituality through Godliness. 2 Timothy 6:6 ***"Now Godliness with contentment is great gain."*** no matter how much you gain in the physical, no matter how much you build up you physical self, without Godliness you remain poor, weak, and vulnerable to the devil to be a victor in your life. Godliness is a wonderful attribute. By Godliness, though we may lose something's in natural, it shall all be made up in the life to come. Godliness is not a quick fix, it is a daily commitment; it is something we continue to work toward every day, it is showing determination to be like Christ in all we do and say.

Brotherly Kindness & Love:
"Finally, all of you be of one mind, having compassion for one another; love as brothers, be tenderhearted, be courteous;" 1Peter 3:8
"A new commandment I give to you, that you love one another; as I have loved you, that you also love one another." John 13:34

I decided to join these two fibers because they basically go hand in hand. In 1 Peter 3:8, Peter is teaching how the saints of God are to conduct themselves towards one another. As believers in the body of Christ, all we do should be done with one mind, and in real love. Though times may come that we are not going to agree, but, that shouldn't become a stumbling block in the relationships of the saints. We are to be compassionate, remembering that we too had to have compassion to get to where we are now. And most importantly love one to another as brother/sisters in Christ.

Now we have discussed love in a previous chapter. Here love is dealing with actions. You can speak on how you love someone all day, but what are you doing or what have you done to confirm that love for the brethren? When we begin to do away with the lip service and begin to act upon that in which we speak, our ropes become strengthened even the more. How? Because when we spread the love of Christ we then strengthen the brethren, anything opposite of that causes breaking in the rope. Jesus said to us in John 13, to love one another as he has love us. What does that mean to us? Jesus loved us so much to come down and take on the sins of the world, to give us the opportunity to come into a covenant with him. He took on the death that we deserved to give us life. If that's not love, to die for someone who don't even deserve a second chance; then I don't know what is. He was persecuted, beaten, flesh torn from his body, he was spat on just for you and I because of the love he had for us. What greater love than this? Now I am sure that most of us would not say that we would die for our neighbor, but, that's not the case always. Are you capable of giving of your life, time, or resources to the fellow brethren and spread the love of Christ. That's what he did for us, he not only gave up his life and died for us, but he made himself available for those who needed him. These things are pleasing to him.

CHAPTER 5

Attitude is everything

"Rejoicing in hope, patient in tribulation, continuing steadfastly in prayer" Romans 12:12

In this section we focus on the mindset we are to have in the midst of trial. Your attitude is everything; which ultimately confirms all the previous fiber we have previously discussed. If we have the wrong mindset in our situations, then we tend to lose sight of the victory. Paul said in Romans 12:2 "...Being transformed in the renewing of your mind..." we are to put on the mind of Christ, in our situations; knowing that we have a purpose of enduring the things we face, though it may seem like we can't make it. Even Jesus became weary, when he asked God to "Let this cup pass from me"; yet he then prayed that never-the-less, that God's will be done. The enemy has a plot, but God still has a plan, but can you trust him in this until he brings a change. Though things may be in a mess right now, with the right attitude; you realize that your mess can become a message, and your test can become your testimony. It's according to how you see things.

Rejoicing in hope:
"I will bless the Lord at all times; His praise shall continually be in my mouth." Psalms 34:1

We need to have an attitude to praise God in hope. Praise should never be predicated on how you feel. I've said before, emotions will often change due to the current situations in an individual's life. I can honestly admit, there have been times in my life where I had been so down and my praise (or the lack thereof) always reflected my emotions. If I was sad, hurt, or depressed, my praise was always "dry" and depressing. It lacked heart and purity. If I was happy then you really knew it based on the praises. Here David made a declaration to "Bless the Lord at all times" which signifies that regardless of how he feels he will always bless God. We need to understand that we can never really praise God enough, but we should use the time we have to praise him all we can. Elect Lady K. Taylor said something so powerful concerning praise in bible study one night. She was talking about how we go through so much in life and how God has been faithful to help us through, that you really can't help but praise him. She then said that she find herself praising God for something he has done years ago. She hasn't really come up to date with her praise yet, she still giving past due praises. Have you ever had a bill that you couldn't pay for the services rendered too you, and they sent an invoice that said "Past Due Bill"? That's what she was saying, that she hasn't paid in full the praises to God for what he has already done; so before she can get to praise God for the now, she had to still give praise for back then. To me she had the mindset of David, to bless him at all times and to allow his praise to continue to flow from her lips. If there is any encouragement, it should be the fact that God has already brought you through a lot, so you know he will do it again. Yet, if He never does anything else, He's already done enough!

The commandment remains that if you have breath in your body, you are required to praise the Lord. So if you rejoice in hope, you are showing God that even in the midst of trouble; you trust him enough to allow his will to take place. Your praise will confuse your enemy and the very thing your enemy tried to do to you, your praise will reverse it. So no matter what you may be facing, GIVE GOD THE PRAISE. Philippians 4:4 says, "Rejoice in the Lord always. Again I will say rejoice!" No matter where you find yourself, Rejoice and again I say rejoice! After all God is still worthy to be praised in spite of what you are going through! Exalt him and lift him up!

Patience in tribulation:
"These things I have spoken to you, that in me you may have peace. In the world you will have tribulation; but be of good cheer, I have overcome the world." John 16:33

Tribulations will come in the life of believers, but through God we find peace in the midst of chaos. Patience in these trials should be easy when we abide in Christ and Him in us. We can rejoice and patiently wait on God, no matter the problems we face in the world; because He has already overcome the world for us, all we have to do is live through it. Knowing that God will not leave us, nor forsake us, though it may seem like he has left our side, he will not forget the promises that he has made us. He is merciful and will bring us out in due time. Acts 14:22 says, **"Strengthening the souls of the disciples, exhorting them to continue in faith and saying, 'we must through much tribulation enter the Kingdom of God.'"** Be encouraged in the midst of opposition, because God will surely bring you into the kingdom, after which you have listened to and obeyed his voice. Tribulations manifest the evidence of the righteousness of God that we may be considered worthy of the Kingdom of God. That's purpose in which we suffer (2Thess 1:4-7). Keep pressing toward the mark. God will surely come on your behalf. Keep the faith, and don't give up.

Consistency in prayer:
"Pray without Ceasing." 1 Thessalonians 5:17

I've often heard that prayer is the key, when we begin to pray, and trust God with what we pray; his ear is open and attentive to our cry. Prayer is simply just having a conversation with God as we would our loved ones. It doesn't have to be long and deep, it just needs to be open and real. Prayer does not always consist of asking for something, but also honoring God for who he is, and praising him for what he has done. At times we may not know the words to say, but, God knows our heart. For out of the heart, flow the issues of life. In those moments the spiritual side kicks in, Romans 8 says, **"if we don't know how or what to pray, it doesn't matter. He does our praying in and for us, making prayer out** *of our wordless sighs, our aching groans."* The spirit of Christ makes intercession for us, in times that we cannot seem to express ourselves in prayer. James 5:16 says, *"...the effectual; fervent prayers of the righteous avail much"*, your prayer has to be real, and it will take effect in your life, and will help accomplish much! We now have the privilege of going behind the veil, and enter into the holy place of God for ourselves. When Jesus died for our sins to make us a holy people; the bible says that we can come boldly before the throne of grace and let the requests be made known. Be mindful to pray according to God's will for your life. Praying in Jesus' name, seals the deal.

I've heard the older saints say, "If you going to pray don't worry; if you're going to worry don't pray" when you pray, you pour yourselves out on the altar. There is no reason to worry once you've given it to God. I have found, a lot of times that I have prayed and picked up the very thing that I prayed about. It's hard for God to work on our situations if we continue to carry them in our minds, emotions, and actions. HE said cast all your cares on me, for I car for you. When you give it to God Leave it there and let him work it out. Prayer must be a consistent part of our lives. Jesus was praying, and the disciples fell asleep, and he came back and said could you not pray with me for one hour!

CHAPTER 6

Model Prayer Outline

The first section of Matthew 6:8-13 basically teaches the dos and don'ts of prayer. Don't pray to be seen or heard, but pray in secret that God may openly reward you. It's not about the wording or length of the prayer, it's about the substance, because God knows everything you need before you even ask. So when the disciples said teach us how to pray, Jesus said to them, pray in this manner:

- Our father who art in heaven
  - This is recognition of who God is. He is our father, the one who sits on the throne and is able to answer our prayers.
  - He's our heavenly father, the one who provides all our needs.
- Hollowed be thy name.
  - This is showing honor to him.
  - Its saying holy, wonderful, great (etc.) is your name. Why? Because we know that his name is above all names. He is holy and mighty. So therefore is worthy to be praised in such a manner.
  - Praise him, before asking for anything. HE deserves it after all.
- Your kingdom come,
  - Petition for the manifestation of his kingdom. He said that the kingdom of heaven is at hand, we should pray in expectation of it to come. Because the word says so.
  - The bible says seek ye first the Kingdom and all its righteousness and everything else will be added.
  - God wants to bring his kingdom to us. Therefore to be partakers in the kingdom, you then pray that:

- Thy will be done on earth as it is in heaven
  - Pray that God's will be done, and that he helps you to live according to his will for your life as it pleases him.
  - Even though we have our own agenda and plans for life, but Gods will must be first in our lives.
  - We pray that God's will be performed on earth as it already exists in heaven.
- Give us this day our daily bread
  - Pray for your day and the provisions he has made for it.
  - Now that we have prayed for the spiritual and divine things of God, we can now pray for our Physical necessities in life.
  - Don't really have to take thought for tomorrow, for tomorrow will take care of itself, but pray for this day and pray for tomorrow that if the Lord allows you to see it.
- Forgive us our debts, and we forgive our debtors
  - Being that the daily bread feeds us, we must be careful that we take care of the un-forgiven sin in our lives, or it would be like feeding a lamb only to be slaughtered.
  - Then we also forgive those who have sinned (in debt) toward us. We should forgive as Christ forgives us. For how can we ask for forgiveness from Him and not forgive those whom we see every day!
- And lead us not into temptation, but deliver us for evil
  - Praying that the sin that we have committed is removed, we then pray for God's guidance to keep us from going back into the things we have been delivered.
  - And also asking him to deliver and protect us from the evil that lay in wait for us. Sin waits at the door and the devil waits for an opportune time to try and take control. But pray God helps you to resist the devil.
- For thine is the kingdom, the power, and the glory forever and ever
  - It is our responsibility and an esteemed privilege to talk with God through prayer. Not just to move god, but also to build ourselves up in our spirituality.

- In closing of the prayer, you are to be sure to recognize and acknowledge; that all things in heaven and earth belong to God, and exist because of his greatness. It is a way of praising God. For His is the kingdom, for he is our King, and His is the power, for he has all power, and His is the glory, which comes through the trials, tribulation, and faith of the believers.
- And because God is eternal, so are his blessings and majesty and therefore so should our praise. By saying forever and ever.
- Amen!
  - Let it be so, it is the seal that you have spoken your desire and you believe in the power of prayer. It is to be sure that God shall and will hear; and be attentive unto the prayers that have gone forth.
  - Simply put, Prayer is important. Much prayer, much power. Little prayer, little power. No prayer, no power. Philippians 4:6 says *"Be anxious for nothing, but in everything with prayer and supplication, let your requests be made known unto God."*

Wisdom:
"Wisdom is the principle thing; therefore get wisdom. And in all your getting, get understanding." Proverbs 4:7

The next fiber I believe also needs to be incorporated into our ropes is, Wisdom. There are so many things we can say about wisdom. It is something that is very scarce in the world today. Wisdom is a virtue, it is an ability or strength, to identify and choose what is right. Wisdom is more than what you find in or books, or is taught by man; wisdom is a gift that comes from God, through the experiences of life. You don't have to be old to have wisdom. It's not how long you've been living, but, rather the experiences you've had while you have been living. Wisdom is going beyond the simplistic mentality of life. We all need wisdom, and the bible says that if you lack wisdom ask God; and, he will freely give it to you. In order for you to get it; first of all you have to intimately know and reverence God, for that is the beginning of knowledge.

With wisdom you gain understanding. Wisdom is key to strengthening your ropes.

Proverbs and Ecclesiastes are full of great teachings on wisdom. Wisdom is far more valuable than money, and will take you further than anything this world can ever offer.

TRUST GOD, EVEN WHEN THE ODDS SEEM STACKED AGAINST YOU!

CHAPTER 7

What is your rope connected too?

"I rise before the dawning of the morning, and cry for help; I hope in Your word." Psalms 119:147

This section is very important to our lives. If you have your ropes made up of the right things, you then need to make sure that what your rope is connected to is strong enough to hold the load. I've seen in many cases things failing; not because the rope broke, but the very thing the rope was tied into was weak and fragile. As a child in church, I always heard people sing the song, "hold to his hand.", the words are, *"time is filled with swift transitions, naught on earth unmoved can stand. Build your hopes on things eternal, and hold to God's unchanging hands."*

I already mentioned a few times that your rope is the hopes of life and the lifeline to your destiny. What do you have your hopes connected to? Is it connected into your emotions? Your house, car, family or friends? Your bank account and worldly riches? If so you're bound to fail. Why? Because, time is filled with swift transitions. The emotions you feel now, can change within seconds. The money, house and car that you have now can all be taken away. All these things we see in the world can be here today and gone tomorrow; then where does that leave your rope? We not only have to have a strong and stable rope but also we need an even stronger and more stable post in which to connect the ropes too.

So where should your ropes be connected? Into the mighty hands of God. 1 Peter 5:6-7 says, **"Therefore humble yourselves under the mighty hand of God that he may exalt you in due time. Casting all of your cares on him, for** *he cares for you."*. Here in the text we are told to humble ourselves under the mighty hand of God. Why under his hands? Under God's hand is where you find his power, Under God's hand you find his will, and Under God's hands is where you find his protection. So if your rope is connected in to the hand of God; it is therefore connected into his will, and when you find your life connected in his will you therefore are now connected into his power, and protection, because you're in his will. So being in his will, connects you to his power, that whenever you face a situation that seems to hard for you to handle; God's power steps in and then you are able to speak in his name and operate in his power over your life.

When I lived in San Diego California, my brother who is in the navy was off on deployment and his wife was tending to matters on his behalf because she had what they call "P.O.A"; which means power of attorney. Meaning, that because she was connected to him in marriage, and carries his name; the same power he has concerning his benefits and things of that matter, she has. He don't even have to be present for her to step in on his behalf. Jesus Christ has been given a name which is above every name; and at that name everything in heaven, earth, and hell has to bow in submission to the Authority that resides in that name!

When you find yourself positioned in the will of God; and your name has been written in the book of life, you therefore have the Authority to operate in the power of Christ's Name. The same power that raised Jesus Christ from the dead, is the very same power that God has made available to us through his son Jesus. There is power just in the sounding of his name, for at the name of Jesus Demons flee, at that name every knee shall bow and every tongue confess, at that name yokes are destroyed and burdens removed.

When you're in his will and in his power, then he will cover and protect you! If the steps of a good man is ordered by the Lord; don't you think that God knows everything that you have faced, is facing now, and will face in the future? I guarantee you that if you just trust him, even though you may be in a battle right now, He will take your current condition to birth you into your final destination.

Psalms 91:1 says **"He that dwells in the secret place of the most high shall abide under the shadow of the almighty,"**. God has a place to cover you in the midst of hard times, if you are a citizen of the secret place. The only way you can get to that place is through prayer and being in his will. Though one thousands may fall at your side, even ten thousand at your right hand it will not come near you, because God has covered you under his hand. In his hand is eternity, blessings, and protection forever more. His hands are unfailing and unchanging. No matter what comes to destroy you; It can't prosper, because you're in his hands. Everything will be alright, because you're in the master's hands.

CHAPTER 8

There's a Reason behind the madness

"When Jesus heard that, HE said, "This sickness is not unto death, but for the glory of God, that the son of God may be glorified through it."
John 11:4

Now if you have gotten this far into this book; you may be saying to yourself, *"I have my rope built of the right things, but why is my rope breaking?".* Well, there is a reason! Isaiah 40:30 says, *"even the youths shall faint and get weary, and the young men shall utterly fall,"* the word "Youth" in this text does not literally mean kids or teens, but it is a symbolic word representing "the strong". Here Isaiah is letting us know that even the strongest people will get weak and fall sometimes, especially when they begin to trust in their strength more than God's. I've said before that a rope is designed to carry a certain weight for a certain amount of time in the position that it is in. So what is happening? You are experiencing a season that is called "Dry Rot" which occurs when the conditions of life has become so treacherous and begins beat up on the rope. The changes in the atmosphere causes the fibers to dry out and now the slightest thing can cause a breaking in the rope. You may have been facing many different trials while trying to live for God; and you begin to do so much and it seem like you only get so little in return. You ultimately find yourself burnt out, from relying on your own strength, Thus, you become dried out.

I've noticed this, your rope will never break all at one time. When the rope dries and it's not properly restored at the respectable times, as the conditions of life start beating you in different areas the rope begins to break fiber by fiber; and it will continue to break. This usually goes unnoticed until your hanging on by a thread. It is at that moment that we begin to fear and question "how did it get to this point?" Well, It didn't happen over night; but it's been breaking and you never even noticed it. For example; you spend your life loving people and doing the right thing, only to find out that you're being taken advantage of, and it begin to cause anger and trust issues, and ultimately cause you to react in rage. Well that's a fiber in your rope that has become broken. Also you have desires that are not good for you; and yet you yield to them, though they may release pleasure for that moment, after the high your back where you started, and you constantly try to find something to fill that void, that's a fiber that just broke. Don't add more unnecessary weight to your rope.

We must be careful not to allow our burdens and fleshly desires to weigh us down. In order for you to properly care for your rope, you must be sure to keep it moist and strengthen by God's anointing. When facing trials in your weakest moments, know that God will be your source of strength. Paul asked God three times to remove a thorn from his flesh, but God told Paul; that His (God's) strength is made perfect in Paul's weakness. When we allow our strength to run out; and take on the strength of Christ, we are then able to make it through the breaking moments in our lives.

Pastor Lowery always told me when I was facing situations that caused me to want to let go that; *"There's a reason behind the madness!"*. There is a reason why we experience the things we experience. There is a lesson to be learned and some struggles to be delivered from. So losing heart is the worst thing you can do at this time. James 1:2-4 says, **"My brethren count it all joy when you fall into various trials, knowing that the trial of your faith produces patience. But let patience have its perfect work that you may be perfect and complete lacking nothing.".** Your trial may seem hard at this moment; but it is producing in you something that will benefit you, for the rest of your life. James says to let patience have its perfect work that you may be perfect and complete. What he is saying; when you face the trials, don't lose hope but continue to rejoice, because the trials will cause you to be perfected. Doesn't mean that you will be a perfect person, because no human is perfect; but it means you operate in the spirit of perfection, and to be complete means to be whole. God will take care of you through your trial.

I've heard people say that sometimes they feel as if they've reached the end of their rope. I totally disagree with that saying, because at the end of the rope you are in your final resting place (heaven or hell). Don't confuse a breaking point with the end. No one is exempt from experiencing hardship in life, without the storms of life we are unable to grow. No matter how intense the storms you have to find the strength and courage in God to HOLD ON until God brings you out. His word says in Psalms 34:19 that; *"**Many are the afflictions of the righteous, BUT the Lord will deliver them from them all.**"*

CHAPTER 9

Dangerous Conditions to your rope

Now let's look at some biblical conditions that causes a breaking in your rope. These are the opposite of the fibers of our ropes. They are the attitudes and desires that weaken the characteristics of the strands. They are opposite of the things of the spirit and the bible identifies them as the:

Works of the flesh:
"Now the works of the flesh are evident, which are: adultery, fornication, uncleanness, lewdness, idolatry, sorcery, hatred, contentions, jealousies, outbursts of wrath, selfish ambitions, heresies, envy, murders, drunkenness, revelries, and the like; of which I tell you beforehand, just as I also told you in time past, that those who practice such things will not inherit the kingdom of God." Galatians 5:19-21

this list is full of evil that causes us to fall in life. These are the things that we are to stay away from. The bible says that we should walk in the spirit, that we do not desire the things of the flesh. The flesh and spirit is in a constant battle, and depending on who you strengthen most is who wins. When determination to reach beyond the break comes in your spirit, these are the evil things the enemy throws your way to knock you down. This is a spiritual battle, and you have to be able to fight it in the spirit. Though we are human, we still don't live according to the flesh as Christians. That's why the bible says, in 2 Corinthians 10:4 *"the weapons of our warfare are not carnal but mighty in God for pulling down strongholds,"* And Ephesians 6:12 *"For we do not wrestle against flesh and blood, but against principalities, against powers, against the rulers of darkness of this age, against spiritual hosts of wickedness in heavenly places.".* Now if you can identify with these things in your life, that's a start. Seek deliverance from these things. When you know the strong man by name, you can bind him and the works that he try to do in your life. Lets briefly talk about the works of the flesh, for they are very critical to the strength of your rope.

Adultery:
"For they have committed adultery, and blood is on their hands. They have committed adultery with their idols..." Ezekiel 23:37

We are familiar with adultery as pertaining to a spouse cheating on the other; however, here the text is speaking of a spiritual adultery which is also Idolatry. The people had broken their commitment to God by the worship of other God's, and their covenant with him by living an unholy lifestyle. They perverted the things of God that he has called holy, and the children they dedicated to God, they sacrificed them to their Idols. You have to be careful not to commit adultery in the spirit, by breaking your marriage vows to God. How do you do that? By allowing any and everything to be first in your life, by relying on others more than God. He and He alone should be first in your life. What is the idol God in your life? Be it money, loved ones, whatever it may be; it should have a designated place in your life, but should never be placed before God. For he is a jealous God. It's wrong whether it be infidelity or idol worship. It breaks the fibers of your rope.

Fornication:
"flee sexual immortality. Every sin that a man does is outside the body, but he who commits sexual immortality sins against his own body."
1Corinthians 6:18

Fornication is sexual acts out of wedlock. Here Paul telling the Corinthians to flee sexual immortality; because, it is a sin against one's self. If you are like me, and have struggled in this area, then you will be able to relate that it does hurt in many ways. The pleasure only last for a moment; but all in all there comes a point to where we experience emotional and mental trauma because of it. He goes on in verse 19, to remind us that our bodies are the temple of the holy spirit, and that we are to keep it holy. The Holy Spirit dwells in us, and he is our gift from God, so therefore we are to provide him with a clean and holy body, because it belongs to him. It is so important because on down in verse 20 he goes on to say that we were bought with a great price; we have been redeemed and bought back from the life of sin, by the shedding of the blood of Jesus Christ. That alone is enough to live according to the spirit and glorify God with our bodies and our spirits. Yes we get weak at times and need that affection, but it is better to marry than to burn with passion. Though sex is a physical thing, it hurts us spiritually as well. Masturbation, Pornography, lustful desires are modes of sexual immortality.

Uncleanness:
"therefore, come out from among them and be ye separate, says the Lord. Do not touch what is unclean, and I will receive you. I will be a father to you and you shall be my sons and daughters says the Lord almighty. Therefore having these promises, beloved let us cleanse ourselves from all the filthiness of the flesh and spirit, perfecting holiness in the fear of God."
2 Corinthians 6:17-18, 7:1

We have to realize that we often times reflect the company we keep; through our action, emotions, and mentality. In Leviticus the bible talks about if a person touches anything unclean that person then comes contaminated. By keeping ourselves separate from those contaminants; we then put ourselves in position of abundant blessings, perfection and holiness. We are not suppose to live like the world, though we live in the world. We are a peculiar people to the Lord; We are to show forth his praise, for he has called us out of darkness into the marvelous light. 1 Thessalonians 4:7 says "**for God hath not called us to uncleanness, but in Holiness.**" A lot of times we experience the breaking points because of the lifestyle we live, or the things that we allow to be in our lives. Stay away from the unclean things and watch God work. *(For more understanding study Psalms 1.)*

Lewdness:
"I have seen your adulteries and your lustful neighing, the lewdness of your harlotry, your abominations on the hills in the fields. Woe unto you oh Jerusalem! Will you still not be made clean?" Jeremiah 13:27

Lewdness is the obscene vulgar acts of a person. We all have been a part of lewdness. It is evil, and God is yet pleading with people to flee from such things. They were people caught up in whoredom spiritually and physically; and he is asking, "are you not wanting to be made clean?". Psalms 24:3-4 asks, **"Who shall ascend to the hills of the Lord and who shall stand in his holy place? He that has clean hands and a pure heart..."** your hands represents your deeds. In order for you to stand in God's presence, you must be purified and cleansed from all unrighteousness. That's why David asked, for God to create within him a clean heart and to renew the right spirit. Evil and lewd behavior separates us from God's love, his presence, and his blessings; And ultimately will keep us from walking in his will, and reaching the destiny that he has for our lives. He sees those things behind closed doors. They very thing you've tried to hide from others, God knows. He is asking you, will you be made clean? Will you be made whole? God wants to bless you, will you come out of sin, and allow him to have control?

Idolatry:
"therefore brethren flee from Idolatry." 1 Corinthians 10:14

Idolatry is the worship and service of false God's. It don't always have to be things such as Buddha and all those others; but a lot of time it is money, houses, cars etc. We have to be careful not to deem people and things more important that God. Paul in Acts 17:16; became vexed in his spirit, seeing that the people had been given over to idols. Idol worship provokes the wrath of a jealous God. For when the children of Israel had began to worship Idols, God became angry. Moses had became angry and threw the tablets of the ten commandments to the ground breaking them. Again, we have to be sure that we have everyone and everything in their respective places in our lives, no one should be exalted above God. We cannot drink from the cup of the Lord and the cup of demons at the same time. We can't expect to live a form of Godliness, and expect to reap his blessings; all the while living according to the flesh. Now, Yes we are human; we make mistakes, but this is not talking about you making mistakes, it is talking about those who make it a lifestyle.

Witchcraft:
"For Rebellion is as the sin of witchcraft..." 1 Samuel 15:23

Exodus 22:18 says, *"You shall not permit a witch to live."*. A lot of times we picture witches as those people in the pointy black hats and long noses with the mole on their nostril. That's a fairy tale, these witches here are those that dwell among us every day. That seek the presence of evil in order to hurt other people. That use their words and actions to entice, seduce and mess with people's lives. Psychics, palm readers, soothsayers, things of that nature are examples of witchcraft. Zodiac readers and things like that. Well, you may be thinking "I am not that person." well good, however, You don't have to be a witch to operate in the spirit of witchcraft. Rebellion is a sin of witchcraft. We got to be careful to stay away from rebellion. Proverbs 17:11 says **"An evil man only seeks rebellion.",** you are considered evil seeking after the ways of rebellion. Rebellion also separates you from God.

Hatred:
"Hatred stirs up strife, but Love covers all sins" Proverbs 10:12 (NKJV)

Hatred takes on many forms; and, it is running rapid in this day in time, and sadly its even in the church. How is it possible for you to say you love God, in whom you have never seen, yet have hatred toward your brothers and sisters that you see every day. God commanded us to love one another; even as he has loved us. We find people hating each other because of one's skin color, financial status, possessions, etc. and it is breaking God's heart. If we can learn to love like the bible says love, a lot of things we face now wouldn't even be an issue. When are we as a people going to learn, that it doesn't matter where a person is from or the color of their skin? If we want to see an example, look at Jesus! The grace, love and salvation of God; was not even meant for us, for we were a gentile nation. Yet God saw fit to love us where we was, for who we was, just as we was, and adopted us through the shedding of the blood of his son. We have got to learn how to love, and not just a verbal since but love in our actions. No more killing one another, or tearing another down, but in building each other up. The hatred has cause so much strife, and it only takes one small spark to cause a huge explosion and implosion. If you watch it, the only reason we experience so much hell on the outside, is because we are so full of hell on the inside. If you don't have love, your poor, simple and unsuccessful regardless of how much money you have, what kind of car you drive, or house you live in. We have to have that Agape love. For love will cover all of your imperfections.

Contentions:
"A fools lips enter into contentions, and his mouth causes for blows"
Proverbs18:6

I can honestly admit, that a lot of the struggles I faced was because of my mouth. Contentions and hatred goes hand in hand. Luke 6:35 says, **"...out of the abundance of the heart, the mouth speaks..."**. If you have hate in your heart toward a person, then somewhere down the road you will begin to speak of that person in hate. Sometimes we need to learn when to speak, and when to keep our mouths closed. Our mouth can get us in trouble so fast, and leave us more bound than when we began. While you are trying to make it yourself, you have no time to worry, or speak on another individual. A lot of times; it's not the things you say, but it is the way you say it. Proverbs 17:14 says **"the beginning of strife is like releasing water, so therefore cut off strife before a quarrel starts."**. Like running water, you have the ability to cut it on and off. Turn it off, because you will find out that everything is not worth being acknowledged.

Even when people are doing wrong by you, sometimes you just have to walk away. Because, at the end of the day you are on your way to perfection, don't allow your mouth to be a stumbling block. Let God handle it. It's not what goes into your mouth that defiles you, but rather that which proceeds out of your mouth defiles you, and causes you to fail.

Jealousy/Envy:
"...for love is as strong as death, and jealousy as cruel as the grave..."
Songs of Solomon 8:6

Jealousy, like hatred and contention is another attitude running rapid in the church, and lives of the people. Don't find yourself looking at the life of another person; and provoke yourself to Jealousy, thus causing hatred and contention with that person. There is a time and season for everyone, and I have found that those haters will be jealous and hate on your season, because they wish it was them. Understand this, if you can rejoice with others even when you are not the one being blessed at that moment, don't you Know God will begin to pour out blessings on you. Esteem your brethren higher than yourself, knowing that your time is coming.

Outburst of wrath:
"He who is slow to wrath has great understanding, but he who is impulsive exalts folly" Proverbs 14:29

When we find ourselves victims to the ignorance of jealousy, contentions, and hatred, our job is to keep our cool. The sin is not getting angry, rather the reaction we have in anger. James 1:19 says **"Be angry but do not sin. Do not allow the sun to go down on your wrath.".** When we get heated, we will say and do things through the heat of the moment, that will ultimately cause us to be in regret. That's why James 1:19-20 says **"Be quick to listen and slow to speak, slow to wrath, for the wrath of man does not produce the righteousness of God."** Don't allow yourself to hold grudges in wrath, before the ending of the day, be sure to speak your peace and allow God to handle the rest. When you feel yourself ready to go off in your wrath, just tell yourself "Turn Down!", it's not worth the consequences.

Selfish Ambitions:
"The former preached Christ from selfish ambition, not sincerely, supposing to add affliction to my chains." Philippians 1:16

Be considerate to others and their conditions. A lot of times in our wrath, or whatever situations we're facing; we will talk down to others to make ourselves feel good, all the while trying to wound them while they are already wounded. It is the same as kicking dirt on someone while they are down. People will use the word against you sometimes. It's sad but true. We find people from the choir stand the the back door, who is hurting and they will try and speak words to you, that makes them feel lifted but burdens you. Don't be one of those folk. In God, there is no competition. So don't try and cause misery on another person, trying to gain some type of benefit for yourself. Let every spoken word, ever prayer, and every deed be real. No hidden agendas and foul motives will be able to stand in the glory of God's presence.

Dissensions:
"Now I plead with you, brethren, by the name of The Lord Jesus Christ; that you all speak the same thing and that there be no divisions among you. But that you be perfectly joined together in the same mind and in the same judgment." 1 Corinthians 1:10 (NKJV)

A lot of times we find division in the church. Paul encourages here; that we need to find ourselves being of one mind perfectly joined together. The problem is, when we are faced with some of these previous works of the flesh, we also become dismembered within our own individuality. If we can't seem to be one with ourselves, we definitely cannot be one with others. It is best that we are one with each other, because we have to be able to lean and depend on the brethren for strength and encouragement. Psalms 133:1 says, **"Behold how good and pleasing it is for brethren to dwell together in unity!"**. Though we are all different, yet our differences should only speak volumes of our unique being; while complimenting the fact that, though we are different we can all come together for the same cause, and that is uplifting Jesus and walking in the will of God for our lives, as individuals and a body! It was only when the people on the day of Pentecost came to one accord; and began to worship God, that the spirit of God fell on them.

Heresies:
"But there were also false prophets among the people, even as there will be false teachers among you, who will secretly bring in destructive heresies, even denying the Lord who bought them, and bring on themselves swift destruction and many will follow their destructive ways, because of whom the way of truth will be blasphemed." 2 Peter 2:1-2

Heresies are false doctrine, or manmade doctrines. We all have to make choices, it is imperative that we chose the correct one. False doctrine brings on destruction. Don't allow yourself to fall for these teachings, or those who teach them. It is a scheme from the enemy, to pull you out of the faith. By blinding you to the truth; he then brings you in to a carnal mentality, and causes you to fail. How can you recognize it? By studying the word and praying for understanding of it; that way, when the false teaching come to you, you have the truth as a defense for your soul. Choice is your own free will, do not be deceived.

Murders:
"Out of the heart proceeds evil thoughts, murders..." Matthew 15:19

Murder is taking life from another person; By killing, abortions, suicide and things like that. This is very wrong spiritually and physically. If you kill someone in the natural, you are put in prison. Just the same spiritually; taking life or the potential of life from another, you are held responsible spiritually, for their blood is on your hands. You find that through false doctrine, and evil intentions. Spiritual murder is even worse than, physical murder. Spiritual murder is killing someone's passion, or potential to reach their goals and dreams in life. Have you shared your dreams with anyone, and they act as if they were for you, all the while secretly hoping you would fail? That is a characteristic of a spiritual murderer.

Spiritual murderers are always negative; they bring up your past, in hopes to choke out your future. They laugh at your desires and dreams to do well. The problem with spiritual murder is; You kill the person spiritually, and now they are trying to live physically while dead inside.

Here is how you identify a spiritual murderer; They never seem to offer aid or alternative plans for your goals, they are always condemning and never uplifting. They act like they "know it all", no matter what subject you bring up; and always seem to think that they know what's best for you! Why do people do this? Some are motivated by "Love". A lot of times, you will find that; your spiritual murderers are those of close relations to you. Your family and friends. They love you, they want the best for you, and don't want you to get hurt or let down. So they want you to be happy, and play it safe; but, the way your faith is setup, you want to step out and find satisfaction. They'd rather you to settle, just to keep you from hurting. Their motives are good, but it still causes some hindrance.

However, there are those, who have other agendas. They shut down your dreams, in hopes to have you help them fulfill theirs. It's all about them, and never about you. Stay away from those types of people. Best way to defend yourself from spiritual murderers, you have to learn who you can share your dreams with. Everybody is not designed to go where God is taking you, so they won't understand the passion you have to get there. You don't have to stop talking to them, but you can control the conversation. Don't always let the left hand know what the right hand is doing!

Drunkenness:
"Be Sober; be vigilant; because your adversary the devil walks about like a roaring lion seeking whom he may devour." 1 Peter 5:8

Drunkenness impairs your abilities. Intoxication comes when a contaminated substance enters into your blood stream, and cuts off the blood from flowing as freely and as purely as it should. Spiritually when you allow the works of the flesh to be operative in your spirit; you block the blood of Jesus, and the Anointing from flowing as freely and as purely as it should. Thus causing you to be intoxicated and vulnerable, and the enemy has room to sneak in those moments of intoxication. So it is important that you be Sober and alert, watching your every step; because, the devil lurks around to wait for you to fall. The devil walks around watching you; is significant to the fact that; he knows what you like, he knows those buttons to push to make you angry, or to make u weak. So he sends things your way to catch you in an intoxicating moment in order to bind you. Don't give room to the devil. Be Alert even to the people you hang around, you never can tell who in your circle may be a spiritual murderer!

Revelries:
"for we have spent enough of our past lifetime doing the will of the gentiles, when we walked in lewdness, lusts, drunkenness, revelries, drinking parties, and abominable idolatry." 1 Peter 4:3

Revelries is engaging in the party life with drinking, sexual immortality, and things of that nature. That was our old lifestyle as gentiles or as a unsaved people. But now that we are in Christ; we are new creatures and have been adopted in to the family of Christ, therefore we are to govern ourselves accordingly. It's alright to have fun, as long as it is in the right way. We can't find ourselves being saved, yet still running with the same ole crowd from our past. Bad company corrupts good manners. Not that you are better than them, but you are different and have a more clear understanding of life and Godliness. Again, that's why he said come out from among them and be separate. These works of the flesh are crucial to the strength of your rope. These things can hinder you from getting to the place of destiny that God has ordained for you to live. Walk in the spirit that you may not fulfill the lust of the flesh.

Now allow me to clarify something before we move on to the next chapter. We all experience "Breaking points" in many areas of life. Whether it be God testing us, or the devil tempting us through these fleshly desires, and/or it be a consequence of the sin in our lives. The sin is not the temptation, rather it is the desires to do it that causes you to enter into sin. These moments are when we become vulnerable and we slip up. These kind of things creates the perfect storm. When God test you; it is not for your harm, it is to equip you for the next level of your life. Now at that moment Satan then plots against you to hinder you from going forward; and he sends the fleshly temptations in your path, and if you lose focus, you will find yourself falling into the traps of the enemy.

CHAPTER 10

The power within your reach

"...forgetting those things which are behind and reaching forward to those things which are ahead," Philippians 3:13

The word "Reaching" is the action or an act of reaching: an individual part of a progression or journey. It is actively trusting God when the odds of life, the current circumstance of your life, seems to be overtaking you. There is power in your reach. I've already said that; your rope will not all break at one time, but it continues to break fiber by fiber, until it reaches the point that its only attached by a thread.

Again, imagine yourself holding on to a rope in the middle. Now, everything you see below your hands, is everything in life you have already accomplished. Trials that you've already overcome. Everything within the grasp of your hands is where you are now. It is your current struggle, your current goals that you are working to accomplish. And everything above your hands is everywhere you are trying to get to. It is what should be a motivation to you to continue to press forward, and continue to climb, until you make it to that final destination. Your rope usually begins to break right at or a little above the place you're holding in this current season, to hinder any possibility of you going forward. At recognizing the breaking points in the rope, it is at that moment we begin to fear and desire to give up! So what do you do, when your rope begins to break? You have to reach beyond the current circumstance.

Think about this, Your holding on to your rope, and you are at a breaking point. Now you're confused, angry, and ready to let go. So you decide that you're just going to give up, and make your way back down the rope. The problem in this case is; when you made up your mind to give up and let go, you cause failure in all the things you've already accomplished. I know that it may seem easier to go back down, because you've already accomplished those areas. You've already overcome those circumstances, and so you feel content in that place; but there is more required of you now. There is danger in not moving forward. Trying to stay in one place and never make progress stunts your growth. Hebrews 6:1 says **"therefore leaving the elementary principles of Christ, let us go on to perfection..."**. Only time you can reach perfection is when you make your way to the top. Going back to bottom should not be an option. Going back down the rope may seem fine, until you reach a point in your life where you want to try it again, and now you have to climb back up to where you once where. Having to go through and relive those moments can be crucial if your attitude is not right.

Consider this, you are hanging on in your current place, and you're rope begins to break. You feel discouraged and you are weak, as we all get in life. Now, instead of seeking God to renew, refresh and, strengthen you; you decide to just stay where you are. You are not willing to move forward or backward; you're just going to stay in this place. You have already accomplished a lot, and reaching that level you want seems to be farfetched, and you're tired of the fight. That's a danger zone as well; because, it is at this place in your life, where God maybe using the trials of life to push you higher, but you see it as a destruction. So now only thing that can happen is, the rope breaks and you fall. Holding on at a breaking point with no intention to move on from it, causes the rope to stretch as far as it could, until the rope is failed. Now you have fell, or have "Hit rock bottom"; and now everything you have accomplished is wasted.

But even when you fall, there is yet a place of hope. After you have fallen, only place to go from there, is up. If you are in this place, all you have to do is look up. And if your rope is in God's hands, then you still have something to grab onto. God can and will pick you up, and give you a fresh start in the same position. All the pain of giving up and going back is not necessary if you just reach up. When you recognize that there is a breaking in the rope, reach up in hopes to grab a fresh part of the rope, and know that God will manifest his word. Psalms 91:11-12 teaches that, He has given his angels charge over us, to keep us in all our ways, and with their hands they will hold us up.

Whether you are going through a testing season from God, or a temptation sent by the devil. I can't stress it enough, that you just have to hold on. When he tests you, he removes those things and people that are defective to your growth; and he will prove himself too you in a great way. You just have to keep your eyes on him, and move forward as he moves. The Children of Israel knew God in his Majesty while they were in Egypt; but, when he brought them out of Egypt, They were faced with a dessert, and being stuck between enemies on their trail, and a sea that seem un-crossable. But God said stop crying, and go forward; now they were about to experience him in his power.

CHAPTER 11

My Struggles, My Failures, My Victories

"For I consider the sufferings of this present time are not worthy to compare to the glory which shall be revealed in you." Romans 8:18

I have had some struggles, and failures in my life. I have made many mistakes and still do, but through it all, I have found that God kept his hands on me; and allowed me to overcome the struggles of life, when I yielded myself to him. I often say that I am thankful that I serve a God that, even in the moments of my unfaithfulness, He yet remained faithful to me.

Growing up as a child, I didn't go to church. My Grandmothers went, but my family didn't. I remember as a child; times I would get in trouble I'd go to my room, and preach to my bed. I've always had such a zeal for standing in the midst of people talking about God, and just being in his presence. The time I ran away from home, I ran to the church. Those were the days of my purity, filled with Joy and no cares. As I grew older, I began to experience the pressures of life. I made up my mind that I was going to start going to church, got baptized at age 9, started preaching at 13. I had a love for God and I wanted more of him. Even in the midst of all this, the struggles were all real.

I was different, never really fit in with anyone. I was that kid everyone talk about, or picked last for teams; because there was no other choice. I was always accused of being homosexual. The pain that I felt, and the anger I felt is what actually pushed me to the church; that's what kept me sane. But even there I had to deal with things in my life that no one knew and actually still don't know. Being touched the wrong way and being confused all my life as to what I needed and wanted. It seemed like the closer I desired to be to God, the harder my life became. Going through so much in life, in school, and at home really began to burden me. I walked around with my head hung down, couldn't seem to be happy and when I was, it was just for a slight moment, and I'm back depressed. I couldn't find any purpose to live, and had no desire to live. It was many other struggles going on in that time, and I had to make a decision to take care of myself. I quit school, got a job so that I could make money, because at that time, that was the only thing that was important and it was the right decision for me. I thought of it to be the best choice and I got burdened about that. I received many critical conversations, apparently others thought I was a Hypocrite because I quit school. When that had nothing to do with my salvation. Jesus didn't save me because I was in school, he saved me because I was lost and came to him. Do I regret that situation? I do, but in life we have to make decisions, and we won't always make the best decision. We often time make permanent decisions based on temporary emotions & problems.

Now, I am willing to admit that most of my struggles in ministry were of myself. I allowed myself to start smoking, drinking and engaging in sexual pleasures in every area. I started partying and though I was still a saved teen, I gave into the peer pressure around me, and it caused me to fall deeper. The more things started to go wrong, the harder I partied till I partied myself right out of the church. Now fast forwarding a little, I began to get even more tired of the pressure in life so I wanted to kill myself. I prayed I couldn't hear from God, I began to sing but yet couldn't feel his presence.

There was a revival that went on, Pastor Michael Foster, from Bethlehem Baptist Church, was speaking and so I decided to go. And every night was a message that hit me to my soul. First night topic was "Nobody even noticed". Talking about when Ahab was in battle; and a solider shot a random arrow, and it struck him in between his armor, and he propped himself up in the chariot and no one noticed he was wounded. And I felt just like that. I was wounded and bleeding, needing help to go on, and instead of finding encouragement in the house of God; all I found was gossip about me and people's opinion on my salvation. Seemed like everyone wanted to fuss at me, and no one wanted to pray and minister to find out why I was in such a place in my life. I knew I had to go back the next night.

Second Night he preached "You were built for the storm". Talking about when God told Noah to build the ark. The reason the ark was able to endure the storm and flood, was because God told Noah; exactly how to build it and what to build it with, that it could stand the test of time. God created us for a specific purpose, and he knows our ever step and every obstacle we face. He built us to stand the test of time. He won't allow us to be tempted beyond measure, and that encouraged me deeply. I felt like I was getting closer to God now. I was compelled in my spirit to get back there the next night.

Third Night topic was "Pain is preparation for your destiny" now I can't remember the exact scripture he used for that one. His reference was the most powerful point in that sermon to me, and have stuck with me all these years. We all have pain and things we experience in life on the way to our Destiny. He referred to Jesus, his destiny was to the cross, and he focused on all the things Jesus had to face, before he got to the cross. Being 'doubted, talked about, denied, and betrayed. Then on top of that, he said that the cross represented the glory, and before Jesus could get to the glory, he first had to go through Jerusalem. The place where he was most hated, and the very ones that was shouting Hosanna in the highest, where the very one who cried crucify him! We all have those people who say I'm with you, all the while trying to take you down. I've had many to say they love me, and support me, but were the very ones who went behind my back and talked about me, and judged me based on what they heard about me and not what they saw. We all have those "Frien-emies" those who portray themselves as a friend but are really enemies. That's Just a lesson in life; that everybody who smile in your face, is not your friends. Jesus was beaten, spat on, nailed to a cross just for us. I knew this night it was time to rededicate myself to Him. I prayed, I asked God to restore and forgive me, and I left knowing that God did it for me.

The last night message was "I can't go back, I won't go back". Talking about after God performed miracles for those who were sick or whatever their case; and when he healed them, he told them "Go and sin no more, lest an even worse thing comes upon you.". I had been restored and in the process of deliverance. I didn't need anything to hinder me, because, I was on the road to recovery. Praying more, trusting God more, and he began to reveal in me who I was. He reminded me that I was in the chosen generation, the royal priesthood, a holy nation and peculiar people. That he set me apart at the time of conception and ordained me to be a prophet of God, and that all I had to do was trust him, because he knew the plans, and he would manifest them If I would just yield to him. Now that I had been restored, I made up my mind to follow Jesus, I can't go back, I won't go back. I knew that; if I put my hand to the plow, and look back longing to go back to my pit, I would be counted unworthy to enter the kingdom of Heaven!

I felt better, but I still experienced situations that pushed me back to where I started. Seem like as soon as I get to my house, it was like I wanted to run away! Constant physical and verbal altercations with my mother and my sister. I felt like I was always being picked on even in my household. I wasn't always right, I had my hand in things going bad in the family, but it seem like every time I was always the one getting corrected. I had become very bitter and I started feeling so much hate for my family and so called friends in the church. My fibers just kept breaking and I didn't know it. I found myself rushing to the Emergency room from chest pains that were severe and I had fever. I laid in that hospital bed for three days; and while I was there I needed God to help me and restore me.

I asked him to heal me, and show me where I was going wrong. I was having minor heart attack symptoms, and they diagnosed me with Tuberculosis. When I go out of the hospital I was shunned from coming to church because people didn't want to get sick, they kept their kids from around me. I felt so empty, and there was something spiritually and physically blocking my heart; BUT GOD STEPPED IN! I started taking the medicine they gave for almost a week, and I was suppose to take them for a nine months, but I decided that day to trust God. I went back for a checkup, They found no sign of TB and my chest had cleared up. And I knew then that God had not given up on me! So where do I go from here? No other place to go, except up. And the higher I went, though I faced more obstacles, but I knew God loved me enough to guide me through. He didn't pick me up for no reason.

Just know that even though you may be wounded, and no one notices, you were built for the storms! The pain you feel is preparation for your destiny, and once you overcome there will be glory after your situation. Remember, you can't go back, Keep pressing forward! I have found out that a lot of times, your rope not only breaks from things you have done, but also there are those times when things happen in life that you have no control over. We experience those times where we lose loved ones, and we have bad relationships that hurt us. A lot of things we just have no control over, and it affects us, and causes fibers to break in our ropes, but you have to hold on.

In my life I've had many breaking situations, but the hardest one has been losing people that I loved. I remember losing my great grandfather in 2011, he was my good friend. The most special part was just sitting and talking to him, and knowing he was happy to see people come and spend time with him, was encouraging. Then that next year my grandmother died and that was devastating. She was the glue that held the family together. She was a great help and encouragement to me in my life. Regardless of how I acted as a child, she loved me unconditionally. 2014 has been the hardest year. My great great-grandmother, died at the age of 100. She was a great inspiration and always had the greatest stories to tell. I remember her telling me a few months before she died; God was dealing with her about me, and he told her to tell me, "stay on the watch wall, don't fight the battles because he will fight them. Continue to do his will and don't worry about the ones who doubt it". I loved that woman. She said, if you want to see me again, just live the life and you will! Within weeks after her funeral my grandfather died, that was so hard because we were still healing from the last death. He used to tell me when I was a child, "Be yourself; before you be by yourself" I never understood what that meant until I began to get older and more understanding in life. We didn't always got along because of my attitude, but regardless He treated me like a young king. I honored that man. Then a few months after him, My great grandmother died. Now this lady here, was my backbone. I'm already hurting from the last two deaths, now my granny gone, and it pushed me to some unspoken anger. She always encouraged me and stood by me. She kept me on my game, and made sure I had my head on straight. When I started preaching she wrote a song for me encouraging me to, hold up the light in dark times and preach the word of God. She always made sure to tell the people she come in contact with, to let everything you do; be real! That was the hardest thing to watch her laying there on life support not knowing if she could hear me or feel my touch.

 I know that they are in a better place, but that doesn't stop the hurt. It don't stop me from missing them, it don't stop the pain, every time you go to the homes they lived in, and helped raise you in, when the memories of the location begin to speak to you.

CHAPTER 12

Hang on in there!

"Therefore we also, since we are surrounded by so great a cloud of witnesses, let us lay aside every weight, and the sin which so easily ensnares us, and let us run with endurance he race that is set before us, looking unto Jesus, the author and finisher of our faith, who for the joy that was set before him endured the cross, despising the shame, and has sat down at the right hand of the Throne of God." Hebrews 12:1-2

So what do you do; when your rope seems too keep on breaking? Just reach up and hold on! Knowing that there will be victory at the end. All things considered, in my life; I found that at the end of the storm, the fight was worth it. I always thought of as a pregnancy; the trimesters have a different side effect, then all the pain and contractions at the time of labor. The closer and the harder the contractions hit, it means it's time to push. Through the tears, through the pain, through the exhaustion; and then it happens, such a release and peace; when mom sees and hold her baby for the first time. The glory of your situation out ways the struggle.

I encourage you, no matter what storm you face, don't give up. You may lose some friends, family may turn on you, but you keep pressing. Paul says in Philippians 3:12 *"not that I've already attained, or am already perfected; but I press on that I may lay hold of that for which Christ Jesus has also laid hold of me."*. Everyday will be a pressing; but, as long as your pressing while you're going through a press, things will eventually get better. There is so much at stake so don't give up.

Philippians 3:13-14 says *"Brethren I don't count myself to have already arrived, but one thing I do, forgetting that which is behind REACHING*

FORWARD to those things that are ahead. Daily do I PRESS TOWARD the mark of the prize of the high call of God in Christ Jesus,". Paul says that I haven't reached that place as of right now; but one thing I can do for now, is forgetting all things in my past, to focus on obtaining those things in my future. Don't allow your past to discourage you from reaching your destiny, but press on no matter what you have been through, and maybe going through right now. Furthermore all the things you have already accomplished, walk in the same mind and by the same rule. Knowing that God is able to bring you through this as well; just trust him.

So I encourage you to stay in the race! My favorite childhood group "The Harmonizers of Jemison Alabama" recorded a song that says "Sometimes I get tired. Sometimes I want to give up. Sometimes I feel like I'm running this race all alone; but then I remember GOD said he'll never leave me! So, I'll just stay in the race till Jesus comes!" Stay in the race, looking unto Jesus the author and finisher of your faith. Who endured being beaten and talked about. Hung, bled, and died on the cross, Just for you and I. Went to hell to take back the keys and went to heaven to sit at the right hand of God. All of that, so that we could have life and that in abundance.

Even through our trials and tribulation, mistakes and all that we face as human, yet because of his grace and his mercy he keeps us. You have need for endurance, because God will bring you out if you just hold on and reach up. You may have to cry sometimes, you might find yourself tossing and turning, turning and tossing, but if you just trust God, even in those moments when it seem you can't find him, He will deliver you on time! Weeping may endure for the night, but Joy comes in the morning. So brothers and sisters, no matter where you find yourself in life, REACH BEYOND THE BREAK, and hold on until God comes for you! Trust God, even when the odds seem stacked against you!

I love the Scripture from Hebrews. Paul is teaching a very vital lesson and we should be ready to live this scripture through our actions everyday at all times. Look at what he is saying. The first thing he makes clear to us is the fact that we are not the only ones who is going through or has been through, that's why we are surrounded by so great a cloud of witnesses, the ones who have gone on before us and the heavenly host bears witness that your storms in life are only temporary. Therefore we have the strength to run this race with endurance. Paul says "Run with endurance the race that has been set…" secondly understand the race has already been "set" and all you have o do is ruin the course! And as you continue to run, be sure to look, seek, crave, require the face of the Lord. He is the author and finisher of our faith! No need to give up. Just hang on in there, keep running, don't look back keep your eyes on the prize!

CHAPTER 13

The Conclusion

I just want to encourage you to hold on, keep the faith, and never give up! Though things may be hard right now, the conclusion of the matter will bring glory, honor, and praise to God and strength, love, joy and peace to you. The goal is to endure the trials of life down here in hopes to reach heaven. Paul says in Romans 8:18 "For I consider the sufferings of this present time are not worthy to be compared to the glory that will be revealed in us." I know through my experience in the breaking points in my life that God has a way of taking what you experience now to aide you in the latter times. Everything you face right now is no comparison for what you are coming into.

Further more in verse 28, paul says to those who are the called according to God's purpose and those who love him, that all things will work together for your good! God is good at taking things that is presented in one way, to bring on a counter experience. He's the same Good who stepped out of time, into time and created all that we see with time. He took nothing and made something. He look at the dust, and saw man. God is awesome and all powerful.

Remember this, God has not allowed the storms in your life only to leave you! If that was the case, there was no reason for him to send Jesus. Jesus came and took on the sins of the world. Persecuted, beaten all night to where he was unable to be recognized. They marched him up to Calvary, nailed him to a cross, and they messed up when they lifted him. Because, Jesus said if I be lifted up, I will draw all men unto me. He hung there on the cross for you and I, and he gave up his spirit and died. But I am so glad that he didn't stop there. The bible says, they took him and laid him in a tomb and he stayed for three days, and got up with all power in his hands. Power to heal, power to deliver, and the power to protect. No matter what you face now, God has the power to bring you out. Though you may feel as if you can't make it to your destination due to the obstacles in life, and the lost of strength, God wants you to know today that "You will survive on purpose." You can't give up, there is too much greatness in you.

God is with you and he will never leave you alone. He stands by your side, and that gives you the strength to make it. That's why david said "Yea though I walk THROUGH the valley of the shadow of death, I shall fear no evil, for thou art with me and thy rod and thy staff they comfort me...."

That's why The three Hebrew boys, bound and thrown in to a furnace that was heated 7 times higher than usual decided to trust God whether he delivered them or not. Just because they knew he was able to do it, gave them the strength to stand up for the King of kings, and Jesus stepped in the furnace with them. That is an awesome note because the king came and saw four people and he said the fourth one looks like the son of God. Isn't it ironic the king would say that, being that it was before Jesus had even came to earth. Reach beyond the break and trust God even when the odds of life seem stacked against you, for when GOD steps into your situation your problems has no other choice but to let you out, because it recognize and acknowledges his presence. DON'T GIVE UP, REACH BEYOND THE BREAK!

CHAPTER 14

You will survive on purpose

"For we know that all things shall work together for good to them that love the Lord, to those who are the called according to his purpose."
Romans 8:28

I would like to take this last chapter to give you an inspirational message letting you know; You can survive on purpose. What that means is, God has a plan for you. Regardless what your situation may seem, it doesn't stop the plans that God has predestined for you! God created you before the foundation of the world and in that creation God already mapped out your life. God strategically specifically designed you for who and what he wanted you to be for his glory.

God was there at your beginning, he is there with you in your current location, and also stands at the end, waiting to receive you. Your life is not over until God says it's over. You have to keep pressing until you get to your destiny. Have you ever been driving your car and the fuel light came on. You didn't have any money in your pocket, yet you made it to your destination. People say, "I made it off fumes". Though you may be spiritually out of Gas, the purpose God has for you is fuel enough to make it to your destination.

Let God lead you and guied you. When you know That God has created you for a purpose, regaurdless of your mistakes, you know that you can make it on purpose. That's why david said "though I walk through the valley of the shadow of death, I fear no eveil" why? Because God is with me, his rod and staff will comfort me. Because David knew how to tap into his purpose. Jonah, in the belly of the fish, knew that in order for him to survive, he had to take care of the purpose God had for him. Though he was defiant, God wouldn't kept him go anywhere until he accepted the purpose. A lot of times, we experience trials in life due to us running from the purpose. I want you to know that you cannot run from God, but when God calls you for a work, you.

So here in this text, Paul starts off saying "For we know" first thing is, you have to have knowledge of God and his plans for you. What do we know? That all things shall work together for your good." My grandmother always said, "What the enemy meant for bad, God will turn it around for your good!" All things, meaning every occurrence in your life, God will turn it around for your good. You may have to cry sometimes, but God is going to turn it around for your good. You may have to give up something in your life, but God is going to turn it around for your good. You may have to lose some so called friends, and two faced family members, but God will turn it around for your good.

Even when things get hard, never give up hope because God has a purpose for you. I remember may 18, 2003, I preached my initial sermon. The very ones that said they supported me, the very ones who said I would be a great minister; where the very ones who went behind my back to knock me down. They said I wouldn't make it, they said I'd never amount to anything, but because God had a purpose for me, I continued to press my way through the pain. Now I have been preaching for twelve years, and haven't given up yet.

Yes I have sinned in my ministry, Yes I have sinned in the church, but I serve a God of grace and mercy. His love and compassion is renewed daily for me, and he continues to be faithful to his word. He hears my prayers of repentance and he continues to help me through whatever the situation I face. God will never lead you to a place that he can't bring you through. No matter what the world may say about you, you have to keep trusting God's plans. No matter what mistakes you make in your life, get up, dust yourself off and keep on pressing. Knowing that God has the final say!

*REACH BEYOND THE BREAK
&
HOLD ON UNTIL GOD BRINGS YOU OUT!!*

For more inspirational books, Check out these Authors.

Treasured gifts from dark moments
By: Kawonnon Taylor

Motivational Momtents
By: Ashley Sauls

Hustle, Pray, & Get out of the way
By: Domonique McMillian

Without Christ I Am Nothing
"His remnant movement"

Get your WCIAN apparel today!

   Hoodies
   T-Shirt
   Rings

Visit without Christ I am nothing on facebook.

Word from the Author

To all of my readers, my Pastor has always taught me that when someone has been good to you; you should always remember to tell them thank you. I thank you for your support in this project. Weather it was your prayers, words of encouragement, or through the purchase of this book; I greatly appreciate it! My prayer is that something was said to encourage you to hang on regardless of your circumstances, I pray that God bless you and keep you and that heaven shines its face upon you; And that God bless you in all of your endeavors. Continue to pray for me, as I grow stronger in God. Stay tuned, for more books to come! I love you with the Love of Christ,

Yours truly,

Minister Cornelius Westley Dixon

About The Author

Cornelius Westley Dixon was born on May 28, 1989 in Luverne Alabama. He gave his life to God at the age of nine and has been serving the Lord every since. Through many struggles, and failure, Triumphs and victories; Cornelius has seen the greatness of God and is continuing to keep the faith in Christ. At the age of 13, Cornelius answered the call into ministry, delivering his initial sermon in may of 2003 he received his license to preach the Gospel gaining the title, Minister Cornelius Dixon.

Minister Dixon has the vision of being an international minister of the Gospel, going beyond the church walls, and compelling men and women to come to Christ. Minister Dixon yields to be used by God in writing, singing, preaching, and teaching all in hopes to give hope to all that he comes into contact with. His favorite prayer has always been, "Consecrate me for your service Oh God, and use me for your glory!"

Minister Dixon is the founder of Kingdom Mandate Ministry, an outreach ministry designed to meet the needs of the people of God both young and old. Going beyond denominations, race, and gender and focusing on the soul of the people. Minister Dixon is available for ministry and is willing to travel to do the will of the father. For more information and booking, please contact Minister Dixon via email bishopcwdixon89@gmail.com or via facebook www.facebook.com/Kingdom.Mandate.Outreach.Ministries.

Minister Dixon is available for: Revival, Sunday Worship Service, Concert & Benefit Programs, Youth Services, and all your ministry services. There is no cost to book this Man of God; donations or love offering are accepted.

In loving Memory of:
Justice "Grand-daddy Pap" Rutledge
1923 - November 2011
Grandma Daisey Mae Robinson
November 1932 - July 2012
Grandma Rosa Kate "Mother" McGhee
October 1913 - April 2014
Willie Gene "Grand-daddy Coot" Dixon
July 1941 - April 2014
Grandma Jean McGhee
May 1937 - July-2014
Breonia Nicole Parks
March 1998 - October 2014
Christopher Nix
December 1988-Feburary 2015

GONE BUT NEVER FORGOTTEN!

"For his anger is but for a moment, His favor is for life; Weeping may endure for a night, but Joy comes in the morning." Psalms 30:5

www.ingramcontent.com/pod-product-compliance
Lightning Source LLC
Chambersburg PA
CBHW060206050426
42446CB00013B/3006